Real, inspiring and practical help from guys who really walk the talk.
Bear Grylls, Survivalist and Adventurer

This is more than a book about perfectionism; it is a guide to living a life full of thankfulness and kindness. Insightful and filled with practical wisdom, *The Perfectionism Book* is bound to change your life for the better.
Miranda Hart, Actress and Comedienne

Running a successful business is hindered not helped by perfectionism. Will and Rob give you the tools to achieve your dreams without the self-punishment.
Mark and Liz Warom, Founders and Directors, Temple Spa

Perfectionism is a disease that robs us of the fullness of life we were made for. This brilliant book explains the disease clearly, describes the symptoms, and points to the practices and patterns in which a remedy can be found. For those like me who are tired of living with this disease and are hungry for healing, there is no other book I'd want to place in your hand.
Pete Hughes, Vicar of KXC, London

In this latest book, Will and Rob passionately yet compassionately tackle the stealthy issue of perfectionism (a seemingly innocuous trait), and expose the price that our souls, our health and our relationships pay when in its grip. But they don't stop there. Rob and Will are unwilling to leave us with simply an awareness of our perfectionism. They share practical tools, strategies and prayers that break old patterns, speak life and truth to weary hearts, and lead us forward and guide us to a different kind of life. Take the time to read this book, because it has the potential to transform your quest for 'the perfect life' into a more whole, healthy, and altogether more fulfilling one.
Jo Saxton, Pastor, Mission Point Church and Chair of the Board, 3D Movements

The
Perfectionism
Book

The Perfectionism Book

Walking the path to freedom

Will van der Hart
& Rob Waller

INTER-VARSITY PRESS
36 Causton Street, London SW1P 4ST, England
Email: ivp@ivpbooks.com
Website: www.ivpbooks.com

© Will van der Hart and Rob Waller 2016

Will van der Hart and Rob Waller have asserted their rights under the
Copyright, Designs and Patents Act, 1988, to be identified as Authors of
this work.

First published 2016
Reprinted 2017

British Library Cataloguing in Publication Data
A catalogue record for this book is available from the British Library.

ISBN: 978-1-78359-401-6
eBook ISBN: 978-1-78359-402-3

Set in Dante 12/15pt
Illustrated by Charlie Mackesy
Typeset in Great Britain by CRB Associates, Potterhanworth, Lincolnshire
Printed and bound in Great Britain by Ashford Colour Press Ltd, Gosport,
Hampshire

*Inter-Varsity Press publishes Christian books that are true to the Bible and that
communicate the gospel, develop discipleship and strengthen the church for its mission
in the world.*

*IVP originated within the Inter-Varsity Fellowship, now the Universities and Colleges
Christian Fellowship, a student movement connecting Christian Unions in universities
and colleges throughout Great Britain, and a member movement of the International
Fellowship of Evangelical Students. Website: www.uccf.org.uk. That historic association
is maintained, and all senior IVP staff and committee members subscribe to the UCCF
Basis of Faith.*

To those who excel.

CONTENTS

Acknowledgments 11
Foreword 13
Introduction 17

1. Perfectionism – good or bad? 25
2. Perfectionism and faith 41
3. Perfectionism and personality 57
4. Changing your mind 69
5. Changing your reality 87
6. Achieving excellence 103
7. Practising gratitude 117
8. Practising compassion 135

Afterword: Journeying forward 155

Appendix 1: Prayers and meditations 161
Appendix 2: More practical help 165
Appendix 3: Other books about perfectionism 171

Notes 173

ACKNOWLEDGMENTS

Rob would like to thank NHS Lothian for their continued support throughout his employment and training. Will would like to thank Patrick Regan and Charlie Mackesy for the insightful conversations that informed so much of this text. Thanks too to Shaun Lambert, Ashley Null and Roger Bretherton for their guidance, and to Charlotte Mulford and Lynn Mooreland for their guest editorial work. Special thanks to the editorial and marketing team at IVP (particularly Eleanor Trotter) for their skill and patience in working with our many drafts, and also for sharing our vision for this book. We would also like to thank those who have written commendations, Jo Rice for her foreword and Ben Dewhirst for his perspective as a teacher.

We are both indebted to our wives, Susanna and Lucinda, and to our families far more than we can say, and of course to our God who has taught us much about achievement and how to excel in his grace.

FOREWORD

I am not a perfectionist; at least not like I used to be.

A few years ago I was asked to complete a leadership profile that measured several leadership criteria. I was thrilled when I found myself in the 97% percentile for irrefutability. I hated being in a position where I could be accused of getting something wrong. If I'm honest, I still do.

This used to mean that if I thought that anyone might ever catch me having said or done the wrong thing (or not having said or done the right thing), my inner world would go into turmoil. I worked long hours and ensured I never quite took all my holiday allowance. Six years into setting up Resurgo, the charity I work for, I remember sitting in A&E one day with a particularly vicious insect bite, fantasizing that it would be so badly infected that I would need to be hospitalized – all so I could legitimately take a break without being accused of laziness. Who I thought was going to accuse me I'm not quite sure. I was reading a management book while I waited because it was during working hours. That possibly should have been my first wake-up call.

But it was when a friendship in my life broke down that my perfectionist approach to life revealed its flaws. For all my coaching, training, prayerfulness, repentance and attempts at generosity, I had failed to convince my lifelong friend that I was to be trusted with any communication or that I was worthy of friendship, and we parted acrimoniously, in a way that was, for me, shockingly unresolved. I had never experienced a dramatically severed relationship like this before; my life had never included loose ends. I was traumatized.

What followed was what I would describe as a meltdown: somewhere between a bad day and a breakdown. I was emotionally exhausted and totally bemused by how all my attempts to do everything right had, in my view, failed so monumentally. After a tearful encounter with my GP, I was signed off work for two weeks. I was forced to get off what felt like the hamster wheel of my life.

In the weeks that followed I tried to work out where I had gone wrong so that I could fix it. And to achieve that, I knew the right thing to do – study the Bible. I remember reading the Parable of the Lost Sheep in Luke 15. I'd read it many times before, but I had never noticed the final verse (v. 7) that says this: 'I tell you, there will be more joy in heaven over one sinner who repents than over ninety-nine righteous persons who need no repentance.' I was livid. I had spent fifteen years of my Christian life (and the twenty years before that) ensuring that I had no need to repent (but repenting anyway because that was the right thing to do), and here was a scripture telling me 'the truth', that I was not going to be on the receiving end of the most rejoicing in heaven. God and I had words that day . . . and for many days that followed.

What I came to learn was that I had fundamentally misunderstood grace. The healing process from that meltdown involved coming to terms with all the unresolved things in my life, and letting go of the idea that I was going to get them all right or, indeed, that I needed to. That single change in perspective provided more healing, joy and peace than any change in circumstance could ever have done.

And that is why this is such an important book.

Perfectionism is religion (in its worst sense) by another name, and it crushes our ability to receive or even understand God's grace. The irony is that it seems more prevalent inside the church – where grace is most discussed – than it is outside. As Christians, we often talk about the fact that who we are matters more to God than what we do, and yet, just like the world, we celebrate those who seem to have it all together. Meanwhile, we turn a blind eye to the perfectionists in our community, who are often clearly broken, who feed their addiction to recognition and achievement through volunteering, without challenging them on their motivation, because it suits us for them to serve. After all, who is it hurting? Well, I'll tell you who, it's hurting *them*.

Both Rob and Will are well qualified for the task of writing this book. Their friendship was established at Cambridge University. Rob went on to become a consultant psychiatrist and was also an honorary senior clinical lecturer at the University of Edinburgh. Will went on to study at Oxford University before becoming a minister in London and developing a specialism in emotional health and wellbeing. They are both high achievers; they are also perfectionists, and both acknowledge that the motivations behind their ambition have often been rooted in low self-esteem and wavering self-confidence.

Far from wanting us to be impressed with their achievements, I know they want to help us to learn from their personal struggles and breakthroughs with the issue of perfectionism.

For those reading this book who are tempted to believe that they are 'just wired this way' and that perfectionism is just part of their personality, I challenge you to really invest in this book. Read it slowly. Do the exercises properly, and in doing so allow yourself to engage with it emotionally, as well as intellectually. Your perfectionism will tell you that you don't have time for such self-indulgence. I would argue you can't afford to risk the meltdown/breakdown that not investing might lead to.

Walking out of perfectionism won't require you to drop your standards, but it will enable you to appreciate and celebrate the standards you reach, and to savour and enjoy your ability to make a contribution to the good things going on in your world. But more than that, it will give you gratitude for the simple things, which is, in my experience, the real route to joy and freedom.

This is a lifelong journey. My perfectionist tendencies are still there, often popping up when I'm busy or tired or under pressure, but I am all too aware of the negative impact that giving in to them will have on my life. I wish I had read this book years ago. Maybe I would have dropped the self-imposed rigid rules I could never adhere to a little sooner, and found the rest and freedom that is true grace. And that too is my hope for you as you read this book.

Jo Rice
Managing Director Resurgo Trust (Guardian Charity of the Year Award 2013, Highly Commended by CAF Charity of the Year Awards 2008, Highly Commended by Centre for Social Justice Awards 2009)

INTRODUCTION

We love to expect; and, when expectation is disappointed
or gratified, we want to be again expecting.

(Samuel Johnson)[1]

During the Second World War, a huge volume of military
equipment and personnel moved through previously un-
contacted areas of the world. In Melanesia,[2] for example,
native tribes became overwhelmed by a sudden technological
and material awakening. They observed US military rituals,
like the flag-waving ceremonies that often preceded the arrival
of planes full of treasured supplies.[3]

Following the war, anthropologists observed how islanders
imitated these military ceremonies, even to the extent of
creating similar uniforms and flags. They maintained the
abandoned airstrips, even creating planes out of trees and
vines to sit upon them. The purpose of these rituals (which
became known as cargo cults)[4] was that such activities might
elicit the return of the cargo planes to their island. This was
no doubt hugely affirmed by subsequent aircraft visitations
that seemed to coincide with their rituals.

The islanders consequently believed that their activity was
the catalyst to the arrival of the material reward they had

desired. They had seen others do exactly the same thing over a number of years, so why wouldn't it work for them too?

Perfectionism is a bit like a cargo cult. We observe others who appear to be perfectionists, reaping the huge rewards of affirmation, success and esteem. We then imitate their perfectionistic behaviours, believing that sooner or later the cargo of satisfaction or esteem or approval will land on our island. We even create the uniform of success and wave the flag of achievement.

Our activities are actually fruitless, but because the 'planes of success' keep on landing, we believe that our perfectionism must be working. In this way, over time, we become even more convinced that we need perfectionism to stay successful, even when we realize that happiness and esteem are more absent than we would like.

What is perfectionism?

There are three common parts to most definitions of perfectionism:[5]

1. Setting impossibly tough goals or high standards that can never practically be achieved.
2. Continuing to pursue these goals despite evidence of harm, usually to our own emotional health.
3. Basing our self-esteem partly or completely on whether we have met these goals.

Perfectionism becomes a cycle of repeating behaviour: when we fail to meet the goals (as we inevitably will do), we blame ourselves and try even harder. This in turn further impacts our self-esteem, making us even more likely to fail next time. However, despite being able to see this cycle with our minds, we continue to put it into practice. We remain convinced that perfectionism is essential to our receiving the 'cargo' we desire.

Perfectionism is not just about being unable to turn off our external behaviour, it is also about the harsh negative self-talk that goes on under the surface, and how all of this is linked to emotional health and self-esteem. There is rarely an obvious distinction between healthy achievement and perfectionism, meaning that to the external observer, the two behaviours may actually look the same.

The Christian life and perfectionism

Great confusion exists in the Christian life about what is expected of us in terms of attainment. We follow a perfect God, our leaders are often highly inspiring, and we share an urgent eternal mission. It is not a big reach for us to assume that we should therefore be perfect, and that we should all lead exemplary lives, mistake-free.

Our work lives keep this illusion going: we are constantly busy, facing multiple demands that require a high level of performance. In both the church and the world, vulnerability appears to be a weakness, and it is made clear that progress must always be forwards. Both encourage us to:

- perfect our internal worlds (discipleship, or personal development)
- take on challenging leadership positions (using our gifts, or applying our skills)
- follow the 'giants' who have gone before us (testimonies, or inspirational biographies).

Hiding behind the defence of 'appropriate disclosure', those up front rarely reveal weakness. After all, who wants to follow a less-than-perfect leader? But the result is that only the strong get the limelight, and only their stories are told. Corin Pilling,[6] speaking at the Big Mental Health Day, said of church leadership, 'If the voice at the front is always competent and strong, we risk a message that competent and strong is the only model for following Jesus.'

We hear many stories of inspiring leaders from the Bible, from church history and from our own time. Our hearts burn within us, and we want to follow in their steps. But the Bible's position is clear – it is in *his* strength and *our* weakness.

Then something happens – it becomes our strength, our struggle. It becomes what *we* can do for God, rather than what *he* has done for us. We love God and we want to do our bit; we want to do it perfectly and we can't make any mistakes. Except that we do: we make one massive mistake. We misunderstand perfection and lose sight of grace.

How to read this book

The purpose of this book is to bring about a perspective shift, from seeing perfectionism as a means to achieving excellence to acknowledging it as a toxic and obstructive behaviour. This might sound simple, but we are more wedded to perfectionism than we may realize. If you have got this far, then you have made a major step towards that new perspective.

Here are two guidelines:

- There are no tricks or shortcuts.
- There is no 'perfect' way to read this book.

To ensure the greatest level of success in achieving this task, we shall lead you through a considered blend of information, theology, psychology and activity. This book is based on the

principles of cognitive behavioural therapy, the leading psychological approach for many causes of anxiety and depression,
and a growing area of research in clinical approaches to
perfectionism.[7]

A thorough review of perfectionism in our culture in
chapter 1 will lead on to a focus on the church and perfectionism in chapter 2. Chapters 3 and 4 will look at the brain and
personality to see where perfectionism 'lives', and then
chapters 5 and 6 will introduce psychological tools to help you
make some changes, and to see that being called is better than
being driven. Chapters 7 and 8 will train us first to be more
grateful for what we do have (because this builds true satisfaction), and then to learn how to be more compassionate to
ourselves and others.

We shall also be asking you to take some notes and do some
exercises, which may at times be challenging. However, just
reading the information in this book will not help you to
experience lasting change: you might pick up a few nuggets of
useful information, but these will just highlight your suffering
unless you follow them up with definite action. Your application to these exercises and your determination to endure
some painful emotions are the best way to support your own
recovery.

You may wish to read this book with a friend, and indeed
we would advise you to do so. You will find it most helpful to
choose someone at the same stage in life as you are and with
a similar level of human achievements.

Who this book is for

This book is primarily for Christians who struggle with
perfectionism and have a tendency to achieve at the expense
of everything else. However, it will be useful generally for

everyone. We are all perfectionists to some degree because we all like to be praised and affirmed. We shall all benefit from the opportunity to examine our relationship with perfectionism and discover a better way to live. We live in a culture where perfectionism is uncritically accepted as a good thing, and a paradigm perspective shift is needed.

If you don't have a personal faith in Jesus, then please continue to read this book, as it is highly relevant for you too. The psychological principles that we outline will be of benefit to you in their own right. If you engage with the exercises, we believe you will gain significant clarity and relief from perfectionism. Equally, within these pages you will also get an exciting insight into the remedy for perfectionism that is at the very heart of the Christian message. Should you wish it, this is something that you can receive for yourself.

There will also be some people who additionally need professional help. This will apply particularly to those whose perfectionist thinking takes up a significant proportion of their day. This is sometimes called 'clinical perfectionism', and is often accompanied by anxiety or depression that frequently limits everyday levels of functioning. We shall give some guidance on this in Appendix 2.

Brave people

Perfectionism leads us to use our achievements to generate self-esteem. Most of you will have been motivated by perfectionism for many years, if not decades. It can feel very frightening to begin to unpick a life framework that has become so familiar, especially if it appears to be working. Indeed, a fair few of us will be wondering about the wisdom, or even the benefits, of taking this journey in the first place.

We want to encourage you to take courage and 'cross the Jordan'[8] with us. A life without perfectionism may feel like a land filled with giants at this stage, but we really want you to taste the 'milk and honey'[9] on the other side: a life fuelled by God's grace and love. No matter how old or young you are, it is never too late to experience more of this grace and to offer some of the abundantly rich overflow to others.

Exercises

1. Spend some time thinking about where you stand with perfectionism.
   a) What is the first thing that springs into your mind when you hear the word 'perfect'?
   b) In which areas of your life do you most struggle with perfectionism? (Consider work, family, sport / hobbies, body-image, faith, or your own areas.)
2. Answer the following questions:
   - Have you been told your standards are too high?   Yes/No
   - Do you base your self-esteem on what you have achieved?   Yes/No
   - Do you value trying hard as a very important virtue?   Yes/No
   - Do you focus on what you have not achieved rather than what you have achieved? Yes/No
   - Do you continue to stick to your goals even when this causes problems?   Yes/No
   - Do you avoid completing tasks for fear of criticism?   Yes/No

   (If you said 'yes' to the majority of these, then you probably have a significant problem with perfectionism.)

3. What effects is perfectionism having on your life? (Consider areas like mental health, social networks, performance at work, physical tensions and stopping hobbies.)
4. What one thing would you want to be different in twelve months' time?

At the end of this book, we shall look at some of these questions again. We pray that by then you will have developed a very different relationship with achievement and with perfectionism (being able to see it for what it really is). We pray you will be on a journey towards self-compassion and self-gratitude, for you are an amazing person whom God loves and whom many others want to love too.

1. PERFECTIONISM – GOOD OR BAD?

Perfectionism is self-abuse of the highest order.[1]

(Anne Wilson Schaef)

A woman, clearly frustrated by a lecture that I (Will) had given on perfectionism, confronted me. Our interaction struck at the very epicentre of the confusion about perfectionism, and it is the perfect place to begin:

Woman: I think you need to be really careful about presenting perfectionism too negatively.

Me: I don't think I could begin to overstate how negative I believe it to be.

Woman: I am a happy, high-achieving perfectionist. So what is so negative about that?

Me: Can you celebrate your successes, switch off from striving and accept your mistakes?

Woman: Yes.

Me: Then you are a happy high achiever, but not a happy high-achieving perfectionist.

This clearly successful woman had associated positively with the term perfectionist. Like many high achievers, it is possible that the 'perfectionist' label had been used as a compliment. By contrast, my negative summary of perfectionism was a contradiction to her experience of being a high achiever – and one with a stringent eye for detail. Our understandings were dynamically different, even diametrically opposed.

While there are many terms with multiple meanings in our world, it is the simple lack of clarity over perfectionism that allows it to remain in the muddled space of both good and bad. Perfectionistic behaviours in their most extreme forms have been left unchallenged because of a mistaken association with success, high achievement, and even faith.

As author Brené Brown says, 'Understanding the difference between healthy striving and perfectionism is critical to laying down the shield and picking up your life.'[2] Rob and I believe much is at stake here, not least satisfaction, grace and gratitude.

How do you relate to the term 'perfectionist'?

Have you filled in a job application form recently? If you have, then you will know just how difficult it is to complete the 'strengths' box. Obviously, you have to put enough material in there to show your competence, but not so much as to look conceited. Under-fill the box and you look unemployable; over-fill it and you *are* unemployable. Nothing, however, fills a potential candidate with more fear than the 'weaknesses' box. Typically, people wrack their brains for something to write, before having the same light-bulb moment as all of the other candidates. They simply write,

'I can be a bit of a perfectionist.'

We may not have done this ourselves, but I am sure that we can all relate to the temptation. This, along with the woman at the start of the chapter, is an example of the confusion surrounding perfectionism: that we would both put it in the 'weaknesses' box while at the same time seeing it as a positive virtue. This confusion can be better understood when we try to define perfectionism more directly.

Psychological researchers Hewitt and Flett[3] developed a Multidimensional Perfectionism Scale (MPS) to help reflect the complexity of both the source and direction of perfectionism. Their research identified three clear dimensions:

1. **Self-orientated perfectionism**: Setting excessively high achievement standards for the self, over-focusing on mistakes, inflexibility (behavioural goal: achievement)
2. **Other-orientated perfectionism**: Having harsh or unrealistic expectations for others, difficulty delegating, offering harsh or overly critical feedback (behavioural goal: control)
3. **Socially orientated perfectionism**: Living with a belief in harsh socially prescribed standards, living to avoid the harsh evaluations of others (behavioural goal: acceptance)

The Multidimensional Perfectionism Scale helps us to see that perfectionism is not an issue that relates only to personal achievement; indeed, it has implications for relationships, health, faith, and nearly every area of life. Each type of perfectionism has its associated goal: achievement, control and acceptance.

People with all levels of attainment struggle with perfectionism, and many of the most successful people in society don't struggle with it at all. Seeking excellence and perfectionism are *not* the same thing. Part of this confusion arises from the marked difference between 'a perfect score' and perfectionism, which is a mentality that determines that no result is ever really good enough.

The key to understanding perfectionism comes when we can separate the mentality from the activity. But this is difficult to do, not least because we still have just one term for both. Some have tried to divide out the positive activity in perfectionism by using terms like 'Adaptive vs Maladaptive', 'Positive vs Negative' or 'Healthy vs Neurotic'.[4] We are going to avoid any confusion that might arise from referencing perfectionism negatively and so use the term 'seeking excellence' to mean positive achievement.

Seeking excellence is an admirable working approach, not just because it can motivate you towards doing a good job, but also because excellence is achievable and fun. We are called to 'hold true to what we have attained' (Philippians 3:16), and that is perfection in Christ – but not perfectionism. The real difficulty with perfectionism is that it fails to correlate to any realistic measure of performance; it is, in our definition, a 'state of perpetual dissatisfaction, regardless of one's performance or the performance of others'. Activist and author Anne Lamott commented, 'Perfectionism is the voice of the oppressor, the enemy of the people. It will keep you cramped and insane your whole life.'[5]

Perfectionism as a default strategy

Many of the people we interviewed in the course of researching this book were positive about perfectionism, primarily because of the lack of any other guiding strategy. The urgency to achieve, 'make life safe' or 'fit in' are powerful drivers that can lead us to look for quick solutions. The solutions appear to be found in the three types of perfectionism within the MPS, and yet far from providing a long-term resolution to our fears, they become a problem in their own right.

1. Self-orientated Angus

Angus didn't regard himself as particularly competitive. If anything, he wasn't really interested in competition at all. Angus was far more concerned about reaching the targets he had set for himself than he was about the achievements of others. He was likeable, thought of as highly successful by his peers, and had a strong faith in God. However, if Angus had looked back, which he never did do, he would have seen that his drive to achieve wasn't usual. 'Usual, however, doesn't win medals,' Angus told himself. He wasn't overly concerned with detail and wasn't indecisive as many perfectionists are. Angus' key difficulty was the distinct sense of dissatisfaction that plagued him whenever he wasn't fully focused on a task.

Six months earlier Angus had been made a partner in the very well regarded accountancy firm for which he had worked for eight years. He had dreamed about that moment since he had joined the company, and to some extent he had taken an all-or-nothing approach to the challenge. Having expected to feel elated on realizing his dream, Angus was surprised to find himself feigning delight at the various celebrations that followed. If anything, the fulfilment of his goal made him feel unsettled, disorientated and disappointed. The period shortly afterwards found him seeking out new challenges to address, fulfilling the demands of his new role and trying to replace the sense of direction that pursuing partnership had given him.

Angus' example above is a common response among self-orientated perfectionists. Even when things are going well, they can be unhappy with the result, spotting things others never see. Dissatisfaction in itself is not necessarily a bad thing. It is helpful to be dissatisfied over injustice issues, deception, inequality and even inefficient service. Problems with dissatisfaction arise when we find ourselves perpetually dissatisfied with good things. Have you ever found yourself complaining about a person, for example, saying, 'They'll never be satisfied' or 'Nothing is ever good enough for them'? These are comments we hear often, and yet when we actually consider their meaning, they are truly disturbing.

The horror of perpetual dissatisfaction is not a new idea. In Greek mythology, Tantalus commits several crimes against the gods, and his punishment is to stand in a lake of fruits for eternity without ever being able to satisfy his hunger or thirst. It is from the myth of Tantalus and his punishment that we

get the English verb 'to tantalize'. This is the sense that what is needed or desired is only just out of reach, no matter how hard we try to get hold of it. For people struggling with perfectionism, satisfaction feels tantalizingly close, and yet, however hard they try, regardless of how much they attain or achieve, it just never quite materializes.

2. *Other-orientated Annie*

Annie was driving close to 1,000 miles a week. She loved the fast pace of life and the unpredictability of her job. As an account manager, she could be called out to a client in Thurso one day, Thrapston the next. Annie revelled in the reputation she had earned for dedication, accuracy and insight. While other colleagues were making their excuses for the sake of their families or social lives, Annie was already throwing her travel bag into the boot of her car. She could not understand their lack of commitment.

Over the course of several years Annie became the most senior account manager in the company. However, she didn't get the promotion to company management that she had hoped for. Her appraisals noted that while she was a 'star player', she wasn't a good team collaborator, often dismissing the opinions of others or playing the martyr when colleagues needed to meet other commitments.

Like many people struggling with perfectionism, Annie had set herself up for early success and long-term failure. Having limited her contact with colleagues because of the frustration it caused her, and having chosen not to invest in personal relationships because of their inconvenience, Annie now found herself a victim of the very thing that had appeared to offer her the edge at the beginning of her career.

Perfectionism is unlike other emotional problems. If you have an issue with worry, then it is not hard to concede that worrying is not helping you to make progress with the issues concerning you. If work-based stress is provoking you to over-eat, drink or argue with your family, then it is not hard to see the negative impact of these behaviours.

Perfectionism is not so transparent. In the short term, the focus and drive that it can produce means that you might well achieve your aims and even receive the applause of your peers. This is why so many of us have a confused view of perfectionism as being neither wholly bad, nor really good. However, while the immediate experience of perfectionism might appear positive, the long-term outlook is far from it.

Dissatisfaction had become a powerful fuel in Annie's life, and yet she was rarely still enough to acknowledge it. Instead, she would describe herself as reacting to an 'uncomfortable' feeling. As people remarked on her incredible capacity, Annie would simply reply, 'I like to keep busy.' However, the reality was that 'like' had little to do with Annie's lifestyle. Along with many other perfectionists, Annie felt *compelled* to problem solve, and keeping her mind busy with things outside of herself was the distraction that she needed.

3. Socially orientated Suzanne

> Suzanne felt constantly drawn to check herself in the mirror. Not because she was particularly vain, but more because she was worried that she might not look quite right. What 'quite right' actually meant was never really defined, but there were a few things that she was constantly on the lookout for. Not having a clean nose was her greatest terror, and she had mastered the art of checking in subtle ways that other people would not notice.

> On the one hand, Suzanne knew that she was an attractive woman, but something always seemed to be eating away at her confidence. If she saw someone looking at her, it was never for admiration, but criticism. She found herself perpetually apologizing for how she looked or what she said. Ironically, her friends thought she was just fishing for compliments, when what Suzanne was really after was reassurance that she was acceptable.

A poster in London Underground stations became infamous: depicting a very slim model in her bikini, it asks the commuters, 'Are you beach body ready?' The advert was investigated by the Advertising Standards Authority after an unprecedented public outcry, including 60,000 petition signatures and numerous protest campaigns.[6]

Many law-abiding women defaced the offending posters in a remarkable counter-reaction to years of creeping cultural pressure on females to conform to unattainable perfection in every aspect of their lives. Social media was alive with rebellious posts and messages of acceptance and unity that offered a glimmer of hope in a culture awash with perfectionistic motifs. Yet this small victory has not challenged the proliferation of marketing that fuels socially orientated perfectionism. Church leader Gerald Coates said, 'Advertising strips you of your dignity and sells it back to you at the price of the product.'[7]

While we all like to believe we are immune to the marketers and advertisers, the reality is that we are not. They tap into the very core vulnerabilities of what it is to be human, accepted and included. We see thousands of adverts each day (particularly in urban settings). These images shape what we believe is normal, attractive, desirable and valuable. Our natural tendency to make comparisons leaves us dissatisfied and striving to meet the new ideal. Perfectionists are a marketer's ideal audience. Underpinning this culture are more than 700,000 individuals in the UK with body dysmorphic disorder,[8] existing alongside an aggressive cosmetic industry worth billions of pounds.

Many socially orientated perfectionists berate themselves as being stupid or weak for falling for the tricks of advertising or the pressures of society. However, despite being aware that they are overstating the threat of not matching up to the socially stated standard, the fear of humiliation is overpowering.

Why can't I just stop being a perfectionist?

For perfectionists, identifying the problem is automatically followed by seeking the solution. The harsh internal narrative is likely already telling you, 'Just stop it!' Throughout this book we shall help you to develop a more compassionate internal voice, recognizing that you are not able (or even responsible) to resolve every single issue that you face.

The idea that we might not be in complete control is not one that perfectionists accommodate easily. Perfectionists are typically self-referencing. This leads them to take unreasonably high levels of responsibility for things that are far beyond their control. For example, a typical narrative for a perfectionist who became aware of their perfectionism might be:

> I cannot believe I have been so dumb. I have been living my whole adult life with faulty thinking. What a waste of time! I should have known that there was something wrong. How embarrassing. I bet I am the last to know. I am going to fix this now.

Notice how we tend to make all-or-nothing statements, assume the worst, see everything preceding as a waste of time, and believe both that we could have done things differently and that we should fix it immediately. All of this is under-pinned by this overestimation of responsibility (something we refer to as hyper-responsibility). This is defined as 'believing you have more control over what happens in the world than you actually do'.[9]

In reality, we are not as in control as we may like to be. We are subject to our experience and learning, and the reinforce-ment of these things over time. In the film *My Fair Lady*, a cockney flower girl, Eliza Doolittle, takes speech lessons from phoneticist Professor Henry Higgins. Eliza becomes a 'society lady' under his tutoring. However, while dressed in her finery and enjoying a strawberry tea at the races, she loses control. As the horse she has a bet on passes by, she shouts in her loudest cockney voice, 'Move yer bloomin' arse!' This classic moment of 1950s cinema is a helpful illustration of how our innate learning, particularly from childhood, can hijack our behaviour today.

Just like Eliza Doolittle's cockney outburst, perfectionism can suddenly manifest itself in your thinking and behaviour. The reality is that perfectionistic strategies for coping with life have been established and developed over many years and, as a result, it is impossible just to switch them off. Rob and I want to say loudly and clearly here, 'You were not responsible for your upbringing, and therefore you are not going to snap out of your perfectionistic behaviours today.' At the same time, we believe that you can find significant freedom from perfection-ism as you work through the tools in this book, and with God's help.

The perfectionism life-ring

To give you more of an insight into why perfectionism is so hard to let go of, imagine you are a child floating in a stormy sea, holding tightly to a life-ring. In a threatening environment this life ring offers security and safety. Would you be willing to let go and swim for the shore?

Perfectionism is the life-ring that children often develop in response to the uncertainty of life. They overestimate their responsibility for adult stresses, and this is compounded when parents unwittingly blame their children for things that are not their fault. Consider parents going through financial difficulties who tell their children that they are 'too expensive', or the depressed parent who tells her child they are 'driving her mad', or the separating couple who tell their child he has 'driven them apart'. Sadly, these sorts of shaming statements are all too common and can be powerful triggers for children to start trying too hard to get things right.

Every perfectionist that we interviewed could see early traits of their current behaviour in their childhood, even if it was less developed than it now is. Assuming that we shall simply 'grow out' of old defence mechanisms is a misguided notion. This applies to the workplace, the church, the family and romantic relationships.

Justine grew up in a high-stress family where she always had to fit in with her parents' work demands. She often felt that she was in the way. To compensate, she tried to be as easy-going as possible, as that way she always got on well with her parents. Justine did not develop into a conventional high achiever. Despite her great intelligence, she had largely opted out of academic study. Instead, she found great satisfaction in creativity, and in due course found part-time work in a design and print shop, and mixed this with her own greeting card business. Generally, she was content and was described as 'happy go lucky' by her friends.

Justine was never described as a perfectionist; she didn't fit the bill. Instead, her friends thought she was 'super-chilled' and things 'just happened' to go right for her. Justine was the only person who knew the truth: that she agonized over getting everything 'just right'. The more people made reference to her relaxed personality, the more pressure she felt to meet their expectations and make things look effortless. Her perfectionism was keeping her from actually being herself with anyone. As irrational as it seems, Justine felt paralysed, as being any other way seemed to risk all of the relationships she cared about the most.

I was really struck when visiting the Normandy beaches, famous for the D-Day Landings of the Second World War, by the sheer volume and complexity of defences that remained some seventy years later. Despite years of deliberate decon-struction and then decades of exposure to rough seas, all sorts of metal and concrete blockades and bunkers still stood resolutely on both the beaches and the cliffs. If you were attempting to storm the beaches today, it would still be signifi-cantly difficult. The same is true of perfectionism: defences that we built up in childhood (often because they made good sense at the time) can remain resolutely in place, causing both ourselves and others significant pain or dysfunction.

We can also become defensive about our defences, seeing any criticism of them as a critique of our character and therefore a personal assault on ourselves. In our defensiveness we often create new justifications for why our way of living or behaving is appropriate or helpful today. Letting go of a simplistic self-blame and developing a more compassionate and realistic understanding of perfectionism is a foundation to recovery in this area.

Perfection as reassurance

Whenever I (Will) have shared a fear with Rob in our twenty years of friendship, he has come out with the last thing I would have expected but the very thing I needed. Most notably was a period when I became very anxious about some trivial thing, and he said, 'Yup, you're definitely as mad as a box of frogs!' I was hoping for some gentle reassurance from the psychiatrist . . . Instead, I got something to really worry about.

I thought a lot about that 'box of frogs' and realized two things. Firstly, our anxieties about achievement, control and acceptance are not overcome by trying to get everything right. Perfectionism offers us false reassurance about life's uncertainties, suggesting that we can control, fix or resolve everything that feels threatening. Secondly, twenty frogs trying to hop out of a box describes our 'madness' very well. The walls of the box are always too high; the frogs are like the multiple problems that seem to need our attention and control. All of this energy is expended, and yet nothing really seems to change.

To risk taking the analogy too far, Rob and I want you to know that change is possible, but it will not come by fixing just one frog! Overcoming perfectionism comes through addressing the whole box, challenging your response to expectations, informing you of brain functions and impulses, overpowering the desire to fix, control or win approval. This is a challenge that can only be overcome if you let go of the faulty belief that there is any virtue in perfectionism.

Leaving the life-ring of perfection behind is a decision that only you can make, but when you do so, you will immediately find that you have the potential to swim free, no longer beholden to its limiting criticisms, controlling fears or crushing estimations.

Summary

We have seen how perfectionism has three main dimensions, focused on the self, others or society. Typically, these lead us to seek achievement, control and acceptance. We have defined the difference between perfectionism (which is negative) and 'seeking excellence' (a positive behaviour).

We have explored why perfectionism is hard to escape from and how it is often established in childhood as a means of bringing some security to life: a 'life-ring'. To put it down, we need to acknowledge that perfectionism is a hindrance to life and not a help. This takes courage, and while you may feel like putting the book down, Rob and I want to encourage you not to do so, but to pursue a fuller and more satisfactory way of living.

Exercises

1. Can you distinguish between perfectionism and seeking excellence in your own life?
2. Which dimensions of the MPS do you most strongly relate to?
   a) Self-orientated perfectionism (behavioural goal: achievement)
   b) Other-orientated perfectionism (behavioural goal: control)
   c) Socially orientated perfectionism (behavioural goal: acceptance)
3. How secret do you believe your perfectionism to be? Do others see you as a perfectionist?

4. Does dissatisfaction have a big impact on your life? Do you find yourself rushing on to the next thing?

5. What perfectionistic defences can you identify in your childhood, and can you see the justification for using them at the time?

6. How do you feel about perfectionism now, and are you ready to leave it behind?

2. PERFECTIONISM AND FAITH

*God is looking for imperfect men and women who have
learned to walk in moment-by-moment dependence on the
Holy Spirit. Christians who have come to terms with
their inadequacies, fears, and failures.*[1]

(Charles Stanley)

In her pioneering book *The Gift of Imperfection*,[2] Brené Brown
writes, 'Perfectionism is a self-destructive and addictive belief
system that fuels this primary thought: If I look perfect, and
do everything perfectly, I can avoid or minimize the painful
feelings of shame, judgment, and blame.' Sadly, many
Christians have adopted perfectionism for precisely this
reason. They sense that should they let their guard down, they
will face shame, blame and judgment from their church
or their fellow believers. Some (as we saw earlier) even justify
their perfectionism with the rationale: 'Surely we are meant
to be perfect, for we follow Jesus?' Others justify their perfectionistic outlooks by referencing those Bible verses that appear
to offer support for perfectionism.

As two people who really love the church, the revelation
that so many people feel unable to be vulnerable there for fear

of shame or judgment is truly saddening. Even more so when you realize how unjustified this is, given the Bible's liberating teaching for those who strive.

There are three things that we want to establish about the Bible's approach to perfection right at the outset:

- Biblical perfection is wholly different from human perfectionism.
- Scriptural exhortations towards perfection have the opposite motivation from human perfectionism.
- Vulnerability and compassion are key themes in the Bible's teaching to the early church.

Healthy holiness or poisonous perfectionism

When you try to explain Christian discipleship simply, you begin to see just how complex it is, and how fraught with potential pitfalls too. Paul's letters often discuss the tension. They describe those who were far from holy, 'sinning all the more so that grace might abound' (e.g. Romans 6:1), yet equally there were rigid perfectionists who were damaging marriages, calling for adult circumcision (as a sign of belief) and creating an exclusive club orientated around religious legalism (e.g. Galatians 2:1–5).

A complex debate about sin and holiness has raged for millennia. Great Christian reformers including Luther, Calvin and Wesley have all written explicitly on the issue of perfectionism in the church, often taking opposing views. So perhaps it is best to go back to the Bible, starting with the words of Jesus.

Perfection

The most explicit reference to perfection in the teaching of Jesus comes in Matthew 5 as part of the Sermon on the

Mount. This is significant, not least because this section of Jesus teaching is the distilled ethos of Jesus' ministry containing both the Beatitudes and the Lord's Prayer. Matthew 5:48 comes as something of a surprise in the context of this teaching, a 'gospel of perfectionism' hiding in a sea of grace.

> You therefore must be perfect, as your Heavenly Father is perfect.

It is the unusual placement of this verse that prompts us to look again. Could it be that having asked us to love and bless and forgive our enemies, Jesus now requests human perfection of us? This would seem highly dubious, not least because Jesus also said that he has come for sinners, not for the righteous (Luke 5:32).

If you look at the translation of the verse in closer detail, you may notice that the Greek word *telios*, translated as 'perfect' here, is far better rendered as 'complete'.[3] These two words are interchangeable to a certain extent; a completed puzzle is perfect, and a perfect puzzle is complete. *Telios* appears in the New Testament many times, but is only translated 'perfect' in this one place. There are also common New Testament words for excellence (or perfection) in behaviour, including *katartizo* and *akribos*, which have not been chosen over *telios*. All of this points to the likelihood that the word has been poorly translated in this context.

The tense of the verb used here is also relevant – it is in the future tense (the future imperfect, to be exact), which means it will one day be true: that is, we shall *one day* be made perfect and complete in Christ.

This one verse, which is used by many to defend perfectionism within the church, is not exhorting us to moral perfection, but offering us a future completion in Christ.

Bearing this in mind, which of the following theological statements do you think is in line with Jesus' teaching in Matthew 5?

- 'I lived a perfect life so that I would be acceptable to God.'
- 'I had a God-shaped-hole in my life, and Jesus made me complete.'

Our moral deficiency and imperfection is not remedied by our own effort, but through having our lives *hidden* in the perfect, sinless life of Jesus. John Calvin said,

> How very abominable, then, is the pride of those who hardly imagine that they offend in the least possible way; nay, who even, like certain fanatics of the day, conceive that they have attained to a state of sinless perfection!
>
> (John Calvin, Commentary on Psalms 106:6)

Holiness

Where does this leave us with holiness? Holiness is our response to the righteousness that we have *already* attained through Christ. Philippians 3:16 asks us to 'hold true to what we have attained'. It is not a means to attain to a righteousness that is not yet ours, nor is it possible (on this earth) to mature to a point where you no longer sin.[4] Instead, it is a human response to what already exists in the supernatural.

The Christian who has a healthy hunger for holiness is passionate about honouring God in response to the 'completion' that they have already found. The perfectionist is trying to win their own or others' approval (or control) by exacting their high standards. Healthy holiness means your identity as a child of God is never jeopardized by your performance or your mistakes. By contrast, a perfectionist's identity is never really established and every mistake is a threat to their fragile self-concept.

Muddled motivations

The difference between holiness and perfectionism appears to be very clear and simple when we write it down, but in the reality of life our motivations are often a muddled mix of both the good and the bad. Our Christian service may well be an outworking of our gratitude to God for the perfection we have in Christ, and at the same time we may be hoping that our church leader has seen our good work and finally approves of us. Muddled motivations are rife in life, and there's no reason to stop doing the good, but recovery from perfectionism does depend upon us having an honest view of what we are actually doing.

> Growing up, I (Will) struggled to separate my identity as a child of God from my religious performance (or at least the public perception of it). The pressure I felt to do the right thing was more than just a response to the love of God. It

felt very much like the love of God was dependent upon my performance.

This pressure and the associated fear led me to become very obsessional in my early teens. I would pray incessantly, confess my sins all of the time, agonize over how I said 'amen' or even thought about God. Going through puberty nearly sent me over the edge as I wrestled with raging hormones and religious piety in equal measure. Inevitably, like many perfectionists, I ultimately became very dualistic; I was very liberal in some areas of life and very cautious in others.

My dualism was really overcome when I experienced a powerful and personal encounter with Jesus Christ, in which I finally realized that his completeness was already mine. Ironically, my problems resurfaced many years later when I was a young minister: having fully embraced grace for myself, I suddenly started wondering if I was 'good enough' to minister to others. A desire to 'perform for approval' started to creep in, along with a strong sense that I was somehow fraudulent and not really good enough for the job. One of the things that helped me to address the problem was an interaction with an older vicar. I told him about my sense of unworthiness and fraudulence. He responded, 'Your humility is false because you think that if you had not made any mistakes, you would have been worthy of this high calling. That is pride. You are telling God, he is your plan B, when you are his plan A.'

Initially, I was a bit indignant, defending what I thought was humility, but I quickly realized that it was true. My 'humility' was actually the pride of perfectionism. Rather than depending entirely in the grace of God, I wanted to depend upon the 'good' in me.

I began to read Scripture with fresh eyes: not focusing purely on issues surrounding sin and judgment (as had been my habit), but seeing the genuine call to God-reliance that permeates the whole of the Bible. I became genuinely shocked at the sort of person I had grown to believe received God's approval, or at least could be a minister of the gospel. I was blinded by halos and holiness, completely lost to the humanity into which Christ was born. It finally illustrated to me that my perfectionism wasn't some great virtue that should be celebrated. It was stealing my peace, damaging my calling and ultimately an offence to the grace God had shown me in Jesus Christ.

I (Will) attended a conference recently at which Archbishop Justin Welby commented, 'If invisible signs had power, Jesus would never have been made human.' Something suddenly struck me about the incarnation – that God had chosen a filthy dung-filled stable to be the place of his coming. Surely this was the clearest sign that Jesus had come into the imperfection of our lives to demonstrate his power to save: we are delivered from our lives of sin and brokenness because of God's love, not because of our goodness or merit.

At the same time, having received God's forgiveness, we respond in gratitude by seeking to live lives that reflect the love and holiness that he has shown us. Jesus is both our Saviour and our model for living. Since he is the perfect sinless Son of God, we find ourselves both fully aware of our deficiencies and fully motivated to live lives worthy of the calling we have received from him.

Christian discipleship walks the line between knowing the futility of our human effort and applying it anyway as an act of lifelong worship. This will, combined with the transforming power of the Holy Spirit, lead to a life that begins to reveal the spiritual reality that was received through faith alone.

The church and the perfectionist

While the church community disciples and harnesses our God-given gifts and talents, it can also be a place that fosters or activates our worst traits and attitudes. You see petty politics, division, judgmentalism and perfectionism there. Just like the early church, our churches will struggle with these issues at times. People like me lead churches! But we gather people like us to worship and celebrate Jesus Christ, who is the only one who didn't have these tendencies.

Thomas came from a liberal family and had a very 'experimental' university life. He was surprised by the truth he encountered at a Christian mission during his final year, and he made a deep commitment to Christ as a result. His thinking moved from an undefined pluralism to a mind defined by biblical clarity. Thomas's own conversion moment had come from considering what C. S. Lewis said about Jesus: 'He is either a liar, a lunatic or the Lord.'[5] Thomas loved the clarity that he found in Christianity; no longer was his life plagued by ambiguity and uncertainty.

Thomas's temperament was naturally perfectionistic. He took the certainty of his salvation to the far-less-clear areas of the Christian life. Thomas found himself agonizing over whether certain thoughts he had were sins, or temptations that he had resisted. He began arguing with the pastor about infant baptism and fell out with members of his home group over their approach to the sabbath. He began to face criticism at church for being a 'legalist' who was immature in his faith and didn't really understand grace.

In reality, however, Thomas's desire to get everything right was in response to the grace he knew he did not deserve, and he felt like he had to compensate for the mess of his past.

Having gathered together in community we have the potential for great honesty, vulnerability and unity, but we also have the potential for becoming increasingly perfectionistic. Thomas exemplifies how easily we can fall into perfectionism despite starting from a place of grace. We can often begin using defensive behaviours in church for a number of reasons.

Which of these do you identify with?

- We have confused healthy holiness with poisonous perfectionism.
- We are filled with shame and regret over mistakes from our pasts.
- We see failure or struggle as a sign of judgment on us, and so want to keep it hidden.
- We are trying to win the love of God rather than work from being a loved child of God.
- We want to be approved of by other church members and seen as a good witness.
- We long for the leadership to notice us or think well of us.
- We sense that we are being assessed for suitability to be involved at a deeper level.
- We see people who 'fail' treated harshly (even being ejected from fellowship), and this makes us fearful and self-scrutinizing.
- We are worshipping under the influence of a highly perfectionistic leader.

Make some notes here:

Leader perfectionists

Christian leaders are not exempt from the struggles of perfectionism. Indeed, the three aspects of perfectionism in the MPS (self-orientated, other-orientated and socially oriented) can all infiltrate our leadership. It is essential to come the realization not only that perfectionism is a joyless means of leadership and a false offer of acceptance and security, but also that it is guaranteed to damage your colleagues, the community and the culture of your church or organization.

The high calling of Christian leadership can increase our sense of unworthiness for the task. We know it is 'justification by grace alone', yet we rarely stick with the 'alone' bit. Perfectionistic Christian leaders often carry a very hard internal narrative that berates everything they do that does not match up to their impossible standards. They can also become controlling of others because they feel the whole community is a reflection of their leadership. They may also try to control their families or children to create 'good reflections' of their leadership. Finally, they may have a culture of comparison, to be noticed alongside other ministries, churches or enterprises.

Sadly, many leaders are completely unaware that they are using perfectionism to assuage their fears of deficiency or vulnerability. Others, however, are more aware that they are presenting a false 'superhero' image, but feel completely trapped. For many Christian leaders, grace might be the message of leadership but perfectionism has become its method.

Broken-down but not broken

In my first post as a church leader, I (Will) became constantly preoccupied with ministry and really struggled to switch off. I found myself comparing myself unfavourably to my colleagues and was sensitive to criticism. As you may know from *The Worry Book*, this culminated in my involvement in recovery efforts following the 7/7 Bombings in July 2005. I had taken my superhero priest ideal to a new level, and ultimately suffered an anxiety breakdown as a result. I was no superhero; I was a regular 'super' human.

It may sound strange to say this, but I am so thankful to God for the gift of that breakdown. It has been the making of me as a minister and the undoing of me as a perfectionist. I think in horror of what the subsequent ten years would have looked like had I been able to continue trying to be a superhero. The anxiety breakdown I suffered was the antidote to my perfectionism because it exposed me to the terror of being 'useless'. I finally had to face the reality that people might not love me, might not value me, and might not be impressed by me. In the event, the ones that mattered loved me anyway, and I finally realized I had been paddling furiously to stay afloat in water that was only ankle-deep. My life was suddenly flooded with the gift of vulnerability.

I still remember with some amusement a dear colleague and great minister who was working with me at the time. While walking in a garden with him during my recovery, he said, 'Will, I have to say that I am so relieved that you have cracked up. I honestly thought there was something wrong with me when I watched you working.'

Christian leadership walks the tightrope between worthiness and grace. We need leaders who are holy, but we also need them to demonstrate vulnerability. Unfortunately, it is much more costly to lead out of vulnerability than it is to lead out of superiority. Brené Brown says poignantly,

> Vulnerability is the birthplace of love, belonging, joy, courage, empathy, and creativity. It is the source of hope, empathy,

accountability, and authenticity. If we want greater clarity in our purpose or deeper and more meaningful spiritual lives, vulnerability is the path.[6]

Christian responsibility

We have important jobs to do as Christians: evangelism, pursuing holiness, worshipping, growing as disciples, meeting the needs of the poor, oppressed and marginalized, to name but a few. These can all too easily fuel perfectionism in those who already have these traits. This is why an underpinning identity in the love of God is such a fundamental antidote to the lure of perfectionism.

Perfectionism thrives when you believe that you are more in control than you really are, which is also, ironically, the illusion that perfectionism wants to offer you. Many Christians struggling with perfectionism fear that they are 'letting themselves off the hook' or 'passing the buck' if they assume less than complete responsibility for everything. To help you with the principle of shared responsibility, read Emma's story below:

> Emma was on her way to the station in the pouring rain to collect her husband, who had been away at a conference. His flight had been delayed by four hours and it was 1am when he called to say he was finally at the station. Emma was feeling both exhausted and frustrated as she drove along the wet tarmac, determined to get back to bed in the shortest possible time.
>
> Just as she approached the right turn for the station entrance, she glanced down at her ringing mobile phone, glanced up at the same time as ploughing into the back of a stationary car at the junction ahead of her. Emma sustained

mild bruising to her ribs. The passenger in the other car suffered severe whiplash and was hospitalized for three nights, but went on to make a full recovery. Emma found it nearly impossible to get over the accident, and all but gave up driving as a result.

Emma's mental review of the accident focused entirely on her glance down at the ringing mobile phone, even though she did not actually answer the call or even touch the device. She held herself entirely responsible for the accident, and dismissed any attempts to make herself feel better by pointing out the benign factors that played a part in the crash.

Exercise

Imagine you are trying to help Emma move on with her life and potentially start driving again.

1. Which factors contributed to her driving mistake, but were outside of her control?
2. Which parts of the crash were definitely Emma's responsibility?
3. Do you believe Emma is justified in punishing herself by not driving?
4. How could Emma develop a more compassionate and realistic view of what happened?

Notes:

A Christian friend was shocked and challenged when she read Emma's car crash story, commenting that she would 'naturally assume complete responsibility for something like that. As a Christian, it seems wrong to blame anyone else.' My friend highlighted the precise hot spot of Christian perfectionism: the overestimation of responsibility.

A better vision for the people of God

I (Will) pray this prayer every day when I am brushing my teeth: 'Dear God, let me fear you today and not man. Amen.'

Our relationship with God – recognizing that he is God and we are not – is the start of freedom from perfectionism. We can see that we are not responsible for everything or beholden to anyone. If the orientation of our lives is to live under God, then we can see our responsibilities for what they really are and not drown in some misguided sense of omnipotence.

The devil desired equality with God, not submission to God. It was equality that he offered Adam and Eve if they ate of the apple, and this ultimately led to their downfall. Self-orientated, other-orientated and societally orientated perfectionism are some of the bitter fruits that falsely offer you a means of control. But there is a better vision for the people of God: Philippians 2:5–6 (NASB) says, 'Have this attitude in yourselves which was also in Christ Jesus, who, although he existed in the form of God, did not regard equality with God a thing to be grasped.'

Dealing with perfectionism is far from 'fine tuning'. It is spiritual heart surgery and will have the most profound impact on your life, your faith and your church. The Bible is littered with the stories of those who have come to the end of their ability to keep up the illusion of control and have fallen exhausted at the feet of a God who loves to demonstrate his grace and compassion. Matthew 11:28–30 in the *Message* version is a special invitation to those worn out by perfectionism:

> 'Are you tired? Worn out? Burned out on religion? Come to me. Get away with me and you'll recover your life. I'll show you how to take a real rest. Walk with me and work with me—watch how I do it. Learn the unforced rhythms of grace. I won't lay anything heavy or ill-fitting on you. Keep company with me and you'll learn to live freely and lightly.'

Summary

This book is not a simple reflection on the problems of perfectionism. It is a book about 'life recovery'. It is a tool to help you embrace Jesus' invitation to learn these 'unforced rhythms of grace'. The origins of perfectionism are a complex blend of the psychological, familial and neurochemical, but also of the spiritual. This isn't just a theoretical or a psychological battle; it is a supernatural one.

If these first two chapters have convinced you of the detrimental impact of perfectionism on your life and the possibility of living better, you might like to pray the prayer below:

Dear Lord Jesus Christ,
I was blind to the destructive power of perfectionism in my life, but you are making this unseen enemy of grace apparent to me. I pray that you would strengthen within me a vision of a life that is rooted in submission and trust to you: overflowing with grace and peace because of the work you have already done for me on the cross.

If there are vestiges of old defences within me, break them down with your love. If I am unduly influenced by the expectations and demands of society around me, strengthen my identity as your son/daughter. If I have been living inauthentically, seeking the approval of mankind and not you, God, give me the desire to live for you alone. Walk with me as I continue on this journey of recovery and keep me company so that I can live freely and lightly.

In your precious and holy name,

Amen.

Exercises

1. What do you believe are the key differences between healthy holiness and poisonous perfectionism?
2. What do you think the Bible really teaches about perfectionism?
3. How have you modified your behaviour in church to affect people's impressions of you?
4. What experiences do you have of perfectionism in leadership, and how have they made you feel?
5. How much do you struggle with being vulnerable? How could you reveal more of your true self to a Christian friend?
6. What has excited you about living out your faith free from perfectionism?
7. To what extent would you like to live by the principles of Matthew 11:28–30? What may be stopping you?

> Come to me, all you who are weary and burdened, and I will give you rest. Take my yoke upon you and learn from me, for I am gentle and humble in heart, and you will find rest for your souls. For my yoke is easy and my burden is light.

3. PERFECTIONISM AND PERSONALITY

His fussiness threatened to overwhelm his creativity.
(Alister McGrath, writing about J. R. R. Tolkien)[1]

The *Lord of the Rings* films divide opinion. My (Rob's) wife complains they are too long (and have too many goblins), but to me they are the perfect mix of detailed plot and graphic imagination. But I struggled to read the books for years. They sat on my pile of ought-to-reads, along with Brontë and Dickens – I am surely not the only perfectionist to have such a pile . . . After a couple of decades I gave in and went to the cinema.

Yet the books were almost never released. Tolkien had such passion about his fantasy world that he invented a complete language and history to go with it, but his 'fussiness' about getting everything in order almost drove him mad. McGrath writes, 'Tolkien became trapped in his own complex world, unable to complete it because of his anxieties about the coherence and consistency of what he had already written.' I noticed this in the books (perhaps the reason why I never got through them), as they contain long sections of poetry and saga as Tolkien sets his characters in context.

It was C. S. Lewis who saved Tolkien, and Peter Jackson's films that saved me, bringing a healthy excellence that allowed the story to flourish. But there was something in Tolkien that defines the perfectionist: a need to be right at the expense of everything else.

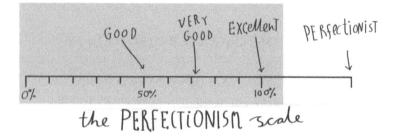

the PERFECTIONISM scale

This chapter charts the perfectionist personality, its roots and its shoots. We see how some brains are made naturally fussy, although 'conscientious' might be a better word. We also see how this can become unbalanced, even to the point of mental illness. We shall also look at the common beliefs and misconceptions of the perfectionist mind.

The perfect brain

Psychologists divide personality into five core domains:[2] openness, conscientiousness, extroversion, agreeableness and neuroticism. The key thing to know is that *all* are valuable, and common, and they are all needed for a healthy society. However, it is conscientiousness that becomes extreme in perfectionism. Conscientiousness is healthy; perfectionism is not.

Conscientiousness is marked by efficiency, self-discipline, being organized and dependable – things we would surely all aspire to. The other end of the conscientiousness spectrum is described in less glowing terms: weak-willed, lazy, hedonistic

– perhaps a key to why some people move as far as they can away from this. Conscientious people are also less likely to engage in criminal activity, and are seen as virtuous[3] – and what believer or leader would not want that? In fact, early psychological research overlooked conscientiousness as part of a normal personality, as it was seen instead as a moral choice and so to be pursued.

However, recent research has since shown it to be a spectrum, and no one end of the spectrum is better than the other. For sure, we do have choices and morals, but our degree of scrupulosity, our desire to 'dot the Is and cross the Ts' is variable, and so it ought to be. A range of expressions of this are compatible with a healthy, and moral, life. One example would be the difference between left- and right-leaning politics, the latter being more associated with con-scientious personalities, but both being workable ways in which to run a country, and neither being able to claim the moral high ground.

Businesses and other companies value conscientiousness – after all, it makes for diligent workers. Other traits such as extroversion and openness are perhaps more strongly associ-ated with the CEO role whose occupants can be mavericks, but all structures need people to keep things on track. Such people are a 'safe pair of hands' or 'someone who will get the job done'.

As you might expect, perfectionism runs in families. This is partly because perfectionist parents value and praise those traits in their children, but perhaps more because personality is in our genes. It's not so simple as being like your parents, as we all know many people who are not, and there are five factors in the personality model above. However, on balance, these five traits (including conscientiousness) do show genetic stability over time – sometimes missing generations, sometimes not. Conscientiousness is genetic, and so is its poor cousin perfectionism, as one tends to build upon the other.

Research studies have shown that the contribution of genetics is significant. Between 45% and 66% of unhealthy perfectionism can be accounted for by heritability.[4]

The fragile tower

When conscientiousness comes to the fore at the expense of the other domains, this can cause problems. This is often based on personality genetics, but activated by our upbringing. We can learn to shut off our flexibility and creativity if these things are never nurtured, or, worse, punished as futile and wasteful of time or money.

In the perfectionist, doing things right or in a certain way has usually been reinforced over many years. The tennis player Andre Agassi tells of how from an early age he was put under huge pressure to succeed.[5] The drive his father instilled in him in his childhood left him pursuing the goal and forgetting the rationale.

He goes on to describe how winning never gives him the thrill it should, and how he worries about whether he has pleased his father enough. He describes how the idea of a holiday is a fantasy – for how can you ever relax when there are points to prove?[6]

Agassi has, with time, achieved the maturity to write an honest autobiography. But this is a common theme in many similar biographies – famous personalities whose foundations were as shaky as sand. We see their match-play and success, but underneath there is a pit of despair.

These fragile towers, teetering on unstable foundations, have a number of things making them wobble. They are coping mechanisms, things we do to keep ourselves sane. You could say that Agassi had no alternative but to assume that his father was right and to succeed. But there's a short walk from a coping mechanism to a denial of reality – sticking an Elastoplast over a gaping wound.

People respond to this in different ways.

1. *The only way is up*

Being perfect feels good – for a while. You get praise for your product/effort/hair, and so the behaviour continues. It's as simple as the experimental rats who press the lever to get the feed pellet. The problem with this is that the same rats will run on the wheels in their cages until they die of exhaustion. Just responding with perfection, and more perfection, and more perfection, could lead to a sticky end.

We've found that all too often, people discover the ladder has run out of rungs and they can't climb any higher. At risk of mixing metaphors, they are now a large fish in a small pond, and this tends to lead to selfish and paranoid behaviour, constantly watching out for the up-and-coming fish who will challenge them for the alpha role.

2. *Magical undoing*

Other people get so far in being perfect and then back-pedal frantically. They realize that it is all a sham, and try to make amends. Unfortunately, they don't have the skills to do so in a generous manner – they can only try to do it perfectly. These people are terribly self-effacing, constantly doing themselves down, and starting every sentence with a 'sorry'.

However, how do you know when 'sorry' has been said enough? Perfectionists worry about this, and so they say sorry again, and again, and again. Just in case. They even say sorry for saying sorry. . . for saying sorry. You get the picture.

3. Anal retentiveness

No, this is not a comment on bowel habit.[7] Sigmund Freud linked perfectionism with being in control, saying that the first thing a young child has control over is whether or not (s)he does a poo. That might not sound very pleasant, but if you think about it, this is one of the few ways in which a toddler can really choose. To go along with toilet-training, or to not? That (according to Freud) is the question.

Freud links this to traumas in life around the age of two or three. If everything else in your life is getting out of control, you choose to control what you can – sometimes your bowels and often your brain. 'Better safe than sorry' is the first step to emotional repression.

4. All for show

Freud also said that people have insecurities because of concerns about how well equipped they are. Yet it's not really about our bodies, but about our brains. It's as if we are worried about how we shall perform, and have to compensate in other ways. Accessories and enhancements are not neces-sarily wrong, but they can be a sign of insecurity or a mid-life crisis.

Self-diagnostics

While most perfectionists are well aware of their problem, it can be helpful to do some self-testing, both to see the range of problems we can have, and also to help people see that this *is* something real which needs addressing. The table opposite comes from the book *Overcoming Perfectionism* by Roz Shafran, Sarah Egan and Tracey Wade.[8]

While these are all valid descriptions of perfectionism, the sixth one (about self-esteem, in bold type and shaded) is part

Question	Is this you? Yes/No
Do you continually try your hardest to achieve high standards?	Yes ☐ / No ☐
Do you focus on what you have not achieved rather than on what you have achieved?	Yes ☐ / No ☐
Do other people tell you your standards are too high?	Yes ☐ / No ☐
Are you very afraid of failing to meet your standards?	Yes ☐ / No ☐
If you achieve your goal, do you tend to set the standard higher next time?	Yes ☐ / No ☐
Do you base your self-esteem on striving (trying hard) and achievement (reaching your goal)?	**Yes ☐ / No ☐**
Do you repeatedly check how well you are doing at meeting your goals?	Yes ☐ / No ☐
Do you keep trying to meet your standards, even if this means you miss out on other things or if it is causing problems?	Yes ☐ / No ☐
Do you tend to avoid tasks or put them off in case you fail or because of the time it would take?	Yes ☐ / No ☐
Score	___/9

of our definition of perfectionism in the Introduction. This is the one that describes why perfectionists try so hard – because it matters! Not the outcome so much, because they know that they will never be perfect, but the fact that they are trying as hard as they possible can, and (ideally) people are saying 'well done'.

Reflection

1. Did you tick 'yes' to the self-esteem question?
2. How would you rate your self-esteem[9] right now?
3. How do you try to raise your self-esteem? Think of both healthy and unhealthy ways.
4. Is your general self-esteem linked to your perceived physical attractiveness?

The problem with basing our self-esteem on achievements and striving is that we fall prey to the '*if . . . then*' rule. *If* we are doing X or Y, or achieving Z, *then* everything is OK. But what happens when life throws you a lemon? Say you break your leg and cannot work – what happens to your self-esteem then? *If* you cannot perform to your usual standards, *then* . . .

The imperfect brain

Given enough biological predisposition, environmental triggers and maladaptive coping mechanisms, actual mental illness can develop. There are many illnesses associated with perfectionism, the common thread being that what is a healthy trait for some and an unhelpful trait for others has, in the latter cases, become a trap and a downward spiral of despair. We hope you are not at this point yet, but we want to flag this up now, as illness may follow if things do not change.

The key thing to note is that right now everything looks fine from the outside. Perfectionism is a defence that functions reasonably well in the short and medium term, yet it protects a soft and vulnerable interior of low self-esteem.

We typically associate perfection with high self-esteem, but what we are actually seeing is brittle and fragile. Like a fine wine glass, it is hard and seemingly resilient, but cracks whenever a significant force is applied.

Deep inside is a human heart that still has great capacity to love and be loved. However, right now the heart is fragile and distant, emotions are denied and deemed to be untrustworthy. The outer shell is doing its job rather *too* well. This model reminds us that there is no point in asking the perfectionist just to have 'more faith' and be 'more sensitive', as their heart cannot respond inside all those layers.

The hard outer shell	• Achievements • Effort and striving	
The soft inside	• Low self-esteem • Uncertainty	
The hidden heart	• Loved by God • Able to love	

1. Personality disorders

The extreme perfectionist can be a narcissist. This term comes from the Greek legend of Narcissus,[10] who spent so much time looking at his reflection in the water that he fell in and drowned. However, there is an important detail: he was proud and disdained by those who loved him.

The hard outer shell described above is called the Narcissistic Defence. Challenges and obstacles are dealt with by an assumption that the other person must be wrong/stupid/weak. It's not so much an evaluation as an instant opinion. The tougher the obstacle, the harder they push.

Up to a point . . . When narcissistic defences are severely challenged, it can all be very messy, with a sudden revealing of the insecurity within. People with narcissistic personality disorder and obsessive-compulsive personality disorder behave in this way.

2. Obsessive-compulsive disorder

Obsessive-compulsive disorder (OCD) is a mental illness in which an individual has obsessive thoughts and compulsive behaviours or thought patterns. It has three key emotional components: Doubt + Anxiety + *Perfectionism*. People with OCD are often tormented by a fear that harm will come to others. As such, there can be very powerful drivers to get things right.

Everyone who suffers from OCD[11] experiences a powerful drive to perfectionism, and they are often convinced that they are horrible people who fully deserve to feel terrible guilt. Unlike the narcissist, they are all too well aware of their squishy inside. Compulsive confession of sins is commonly seen in Christians with OCD as a means of escaping the powerful anxiety that a sufferer feels. However, no amount of confession and reassurance is enough to resolve the matter, and doubts always recur.

3. Eating disorders

Perfectionistic traits are common here. When the emotional wheels are coming off, our food intake is something we can control relatively easily. It works too in the short term – not eating damps down the emotions. But this is not a healthy way to engage with life, and the behaviour itself is addictive. It is repeated, despite evidence of harm. Change is resisted – often talked about but rarely put into practice.

> If your Body Mass Index is less than 18, or you are vomiting regularly, then please see your GP urgently (if you haven't already),[12] as you may have a serious eating disorder.

People sometimes ask whether they should tackle the perfectionism or the eating disorder first. It depends partly on whether the eating disorder is having medical consequences (your GP will be able to tell you), but sometimes tackling a root cause of perfectionism will unravel a more moderate illness.

4. Alcohol/drugs/relationships

Perfectionists use a variety of coping mechanisms to keep up the pretence. Drug and alcohol misuse is common, and individuals can get away with it for years before being found out. Moderate drinking is justified as helping to give people the edge or to wind down after a busy day at the office.

Relationships are also typically distorted. Psychiatrist Richard Winter describes such people as 'a great asset in their workplace, but a disaster in their relationships'.[13] Perfectionists often say that they feel as though they use people. They don't always mean to, but they don't really know how to love people genuinely instead.

Summary

Once someone starts down the road of perfectionism, things gather speed. They become cut off from their inner worlds; they believe perfectionism is helping them succeed; they run faster and faster – and those around them cheer. It is a self-fulfilling prophecy.

Some people try to defend their perfectionism, arguing that it is acceptable, given the difficult start they had in life or the hardships they had to overcome to succeed. In fact, it is not the start or the cause that is important. Instead, it is what keeps perfectionism going that we need to address. This is how we shall melt the outer shell.

Exercises

1. Take a simple personality test based on the Five Factor model, such as www.personalitytest.org.uk. What were the results?
2. What stuck you most from Andre Agassi's story? Did anything resonate with your own upbringing?
3. Does it surprise you that unhealthy perfectionism can be so genetic? Does that change how you feel?
4. What are your thoughts on the hard-outer-shell mode? What 'hard' traits do you display? How in touch with your heart are you, and how does this affect your faith?
5. Have you begun to misuse alcohol/drugs/food/relationships? Do you need to talk to someone about this, such as a counsellor or your GP?

4. CHANGING YOUR MIND

When we are no longer able to change a situation, we are challenged to change ourselves.

(Victor Frankl)[1]

Victor Frankl spent much of the Second World War in a German concentration camp. His situation was obviously far from perfect, and he was equally far from being able to make it perfect. As these external circumstances were completely out of his control, he had to change his own mind and heart instead.

This is an extreme version of the journey every perfection-ist must take – to change the inner world, because the outer world cannot be optimized any more. You may feel frustrated that you are unable to achieve your goals, but it may be that your difficult circumstances will prompt you to make the most life-giving heart change of all.

The Bible, especially the teachings of Jesus and Paul, are filled with examples of people who can't cut back on what they are doing: a soldier fighting a battle, a farmer gathering in his crops, an athlete in a competition. All are told to run the race marked out for them (see 2 Timothy 4:7). Modern examples might be:

- a CEO of a growing firm who needs to obtain the investment to expand
- a single parent of four active and inquisitive children
- a once super-fit athlete who still wants to train and coach
- the leader of a large and influential church who wants to help people be transformed
- a marathon runner who is not yet halfway through.

Books on the work-life balance are typically ineffectual for perfectionists (and high achievers in general), not least because their mentality is infinitely more important than their circumstances. Without the mental will to live differently, no amount of card shuffling will make a difference.

Richard Branson is one of the world's most successful entrepreneurs. He owns a vast fortune and yet has just as much enthusiasm for his work today as when he first started out in business. Branson does not seek to create an enforced life-balance, nor does he appear to be overly concerned about making everything perfect. Writing for Entrepreneur.com,[2] he says, 'Whilst some people try to deal with the stresses of entrepreneurship by setting a strict routine that covers the bare minimum – eating, sleeping and perhaps a little exercise – I am not able to share my own routine because I don't have one, since I try to make every day unique. If you love life and live it to the fullest, there are limitless ways to spend your time.' It is clear that a core element of Branson's success has been his ability to avoid the perfectionism trap, living every day in the moment and with deep confidence in his own unique skills and gifts.

You may think you can achieve perfection or enforce a strictly balanced routine upon yourself, but actually you are as trapped as Frankl in his camp. It's not about enforcing balance, since that will not help the perfectionist. Nor is it about perfection, as that belongs to Jesus. It is, however, about the way we think about success, and the behaviours we exhibit when put to the test. These next two chapters will pick up on these two things.

I like being perfect because . . .

Perfectionism has both positive and negative aspects, so we need to take an objective view. But it's not just about coming up with an equation, as a perfectionist will easily balance this out. It's about engaging the heart as well, to find the motivation for change and the emotion to fuel the fire.

As we know, perfectionists tend to have lots of positive beliefs about perfectionism, believing it to be a good thing. Look at the list of benefits of perfectionism in the table on page 72.

- Which of these do you agree with? Make some notes.
- Rate them 1 to 5, with 1 being the one you see most in yourself.
- Add your own benefit. Is this the one that drives you most?

We can believe these things quite strongly, but this is not just because we are sold them all the time in media and adverts. They also have a function. They cover up some things that we don't like ourselves. You may have noted the phrases in the first column of the table hinting at this.

Benefit	Notes	Is this you?	Ranking 1–5
Perfectionism gives me a set of goals to work towards each day; it keeps me focused.		Yes ☐ / No ☐	
Perfectionism has got me where I am: job / money / recognition. I can't imagine having less.		Yes ☐ / No ☐	
Perfectionism keeps me away from being idle and frivolous / awkward in social situations.		Yes ☐ / No ☐	
Perfectionism has helped me overcome a weakness I have. I'm not that good at things otherwise.		Yes ☐ / No ☐	
Perfectionism keeps me pure so I can do all that God wants me to do. People are depending on me.		Yes ☐ / No ☐	
Perfectionism . . . (*your benefit here*)			

1. Cover up for . . . the fear of mediocrity

'If I'm not perfect, then I will be average' is a big driver for some people. This could be because they were not noticed by their parents (who were probably off pursuing their own over-achieving lives), or because they achieved a lot of notice for some particular thing (common among sports people who achieve young, and sport becomes their life).

Average is probably fine – after all, if you are average you are still better than 50% of people. But for many readers of this book, in the middle is not a place they want to be. They want to do lots for God. But let's make sure that it is glory for God that drives us, not a fear of not being noticed.

We can, however, learn from what it might feel like to be average. Being comfortable with being in the middle requires someone to love you and listen to you just where you are. If you have never been loved unconditionally, then it is unlikely that you will be able to rest easily. We shall cover this issue more in the last two chapters, but for now let it suffice to know that love *is* available, and we can learn to feel loved.

Two famous baseball players were walking down the street. Their kids were in the same school and at the stage of just trying out some sports.

'How's little Jimmy shaping up at football? I bet he has your two left feet!'

'He's getting really fast – I'm struggling to keep up.'

[Pause]

'How's little Jimmy at baseball – any home runs yet?'

'Oh, you know, he's about average, I guess.'

[Pause]

'Excellent . . .'[3]

2. Cover up for . . . the fear of criticism

Many perfectionists equate being loved with their good performance. As a result, criticism can become a huge threat to them, not because of what it says about their work, but because of what it says about them. To say, 'That was poor work' to a perfectionist could be heard as, 'You are unacceptable and unloved.' No wonder they work exceptionally hard to ensure that they will not face any criticism, and become incredibly defensive should they receive some.

The fear of criticism has many negative ramifications, including:

- shying away from challenging opportunities for fear of failure
- being a poor collaborator who is unable to formulate working ideas with others
- needing to be 'right' in romantic relationships, and so becoming controlling
- becoming overly image conscious and concerned with blending in
- becoming frozen in routines that are familiar and minimize risk of exposure.

3. Cover up for . . . the fear of uncertainty

Perfectionism and its rigid rules offer a seeming serenity in our uncertain world. If every minute of every day is filled with pursuing our goals, then there is no time for sitting around making other decisions. For some, this also offers a plausible excuse not to go to social events like the office party. They say they are too busy – the reality is they would love to go and love to have fun, but can't do so because of fears about missed deadlines, their lack of social chit-chat, and not even knowing how to let their hair down.

Sarah is a character in the 2003 film *Love Actually*.[4] Her brother is in a psychiatric hospital and he often phones her, threatening to harm himself if she will not come and visit him immediately. This has got to the point where she has actually forgotten how to relax and have any fun, even to the point of avoiding the romantic pursuit of office-beau Karl.

Working hard and staying late at her desk offer a socially acceptable defence for someone whose life is completely on hold.

I hate being perfect because . . .

Behind the everyday belief in the value of perfectionism, there are occasional moments of insight. These can be pretty brutal, of the 'what on earth am I doing with my life?' type, and so we suppress them and hide them away. But they need to be drawn out into the open.

Consider these parts of your mental health. Which of these do you have problems with? Tick those that apply.

- **Feelings:** Anxiety ☐, Depression ☐
- **Bodily sensations:** Muscle tension ☐, Poor sleep ☐, Nausea ☐, Loose bowels ☐, Tiredness ☐
- **Brain function:** Poor concentration ☐, Worry ☐, Low self-esteem ☐
- **Behaviours:** Self-isolating ☐, Avoidance ☐, Over-exercising ☐, Narrow hobbies ☐

Notes:

Another way to think about this is to consider what would happen to these things if you could click your fingers and just relax for a moment. This book is not about relaxing or doing less (because often that is not possible), but the pleasant emotions we associate with this can be achieved even in the midst of a pressured life.

Can you also see how these parts of your mental health are linked? For example, if you are alone one evening (behaviour), you may start to worry (brain function) and become anxious (feeling), and so find it hard to get off to sleep. Or your low self-esteem (brain function) may have been triggered by an off-the-cuff comment at work that led to a time of depression (feeling) and feeling tired (bodily sensation), and so you self-isolate (behaviour). Cognitive behavioural therapy encourages us to consider how these interrelate. Can you think of an example from the last week? Write what happened in the boxes below, and try to be as specific as possible.

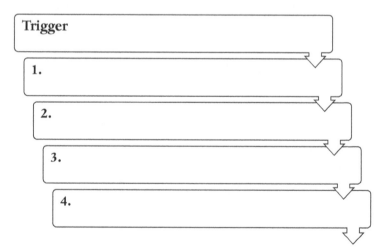

Trigger

1.

2.

3.

4.

- Was there a trigger?
- What came next? Was it a feeling, sensation, brain activity or a behaviour?

- What came after that? And after that?
- Don't ask why – just ask: 'What came next?'

My perfect circle

The exercise above asks you to put things in an orderly line. It is worth spending some time thinking through a situation like this, but we can also stand back and see the vicious *circles* of perfectionism. These circles happen because the things we do (to try to get the best outcome) actually make it worse and fuel the flames of critical thinking.

Two cycles are given below. These are based on the accepted cognitive behavioural model for perfectionism developed by Roz Shafran and colleagues.[5] The key thing here is that in both cycles, self-esteem is based on striving *and* achievement.

In the first cycle, there is seeming success. But because achievement alone is not enough as it must be striven for too, standards are then reset at a higher level. This is what you see in 'achieving' perfectionists who are still holding it all

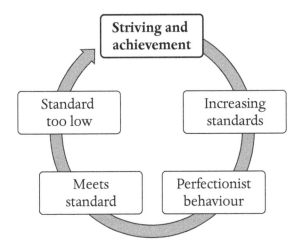

The 'achieving' perfectionist's circle

together – for now. The ladder just keeps on going upwards, and they cannot see the things they have already achieved.

In the second circle, the standard is not met, or the standard is avoided (for example, by procrastination), or the standard is met for a while, but then life happens. Self-criticism lowers self-esteem further, and so even more striving/achievement is needed. Self-esteem becomes lower and lower, so the goals are applied even more rigidly with critical self-examination for possible weaknesses. The achieving perfectionist believes success is just around the corner, whereas in fact the wheels are starting to come off, and performance is actually *decreasing*.

The 'failing' perfectionist's circle

Each person's circle will be specific to them, as we are all different. Can you have a go at drawing your own circle? Consider what is the main thing that drives your self-esteem (1), what you are aiming for (2), what you do to get there (3), whether you achieve this or fail to achieve it or avoid it (4) and, lastly, how you think about yourself as a result (5), and how this affects your self-esteem.

- This is a tricky exercise, so take your time and have a few attempts on a blank piece of paper.
- There is no right answer, and it does not have to be a perfect circle. It may even branch or involve four or six stages. It doesn't actually matter if your statements do not fit in the boxes below.

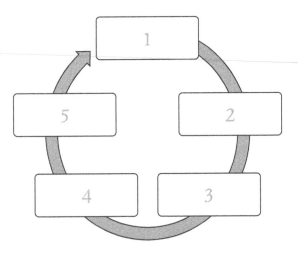

Your perfectionist's circle

I'm worried about change because . . .

Change is terrifying. You may not like what you have seen so far in this chapter, but that's because the familiar seems safer. It can feel better to hang onto a rather scratchy blanket because at least it is a blanket – whereas to let go might mean there is no blanket at all . . .

One common misconception about challenging perfectionism is that this will result in a lowering of standards. This is not the case. In fact, as the 'failing' perfectionist above shows, standards are actually slipping *because* of perfectionism, and dealing with it will enable you to do *more*, not less. However, people can worry that if they start to change, they will become lazy, lose their job, or even fall apart completely and go mad. Actor Michael J. Fox said, 'I am careful not to confuse excellence with perfection. Excellence I can reach for; perfection is God's business.'[6]

> **Remember:** This book is not about lowering your standards.

We have written a whole chapter (5) on what changing might look like. The opposite of perfectionism is not imperfection, but *flexibility*.

The fact that you are reading this book at all must mean that part of you (even just a very small part of you) has some concerns and has begun to see the cracks.

- What thoughts come into your head when you think about the benefits of change?
- Was there a particular event that led you to reconsider your perfectionism?

Now, consider what things might be like if you were to have less of a problem with perfectionism. Imagine for a moment you could fast-forward six or twelve months to a brand new start.

- Which area of your life would look most different? This is quite a scary thought, as it might look very different, but focus here on the positives.
- What effect would being less perfectionistic (not less perfect!) have on your social life, work, spiritual life, your health and fitness, etc.?

Lastly, how confident do you feel about making changes for the better? We should be clear about the cost of change, but also of the cost of not changing.

- What will happen in the future if you do not change?
- What might go wrong if you do try to make changes? What are you scared of?
- Who is there in your life who could help you with this – maybe someone you could read this book with?

Notes from the questions above:
Someone I could read this book with:

_____

_____

When am I going to talk to them?

_____

_____

Myth management

It's important to be in possession of the facts, as responding to inaccurate information is a common driver for perfectionism. We all know that 50% of statistics are made up on the spot, and that not everything on the Internet's one billion websites is gospel truth – but still we get led astray.

What common myths are you in danger of believing? These could be family 'truths' that were often on your parents' lips, or things you have picked up since. Examples are:

- You need a 'proper' job, not one of those 'creative' ones.
- Ninety per cent of opinions of someone are made up from a first impression, so always do your best.
- Good things come to those who – work hard!
- Successful people are the happiest. You need to succeed.

Your myth: _____

Your myth: _____

What would you add to the list? Do you agree or disagree with these? Many people agree with the statement about first impressions, and there is indeed some research backing this up.[7] However, if you move slightly beyond Google and Wikipedia, you will also find some high-quality research that suggests few people notice if an entire person is replaced by someone who looks nothing like them![8]

It can be hard to know who is right where urban myths are concerned, but a crucial thing in perfectionism is to ask, 'Are we any different from our friends?' It is how we think about, and respond to, facts and situations that marks out the perfectionist, not whether we are actually right or wrong. Likewise, this is not about us relaxing our standards below what is acceptable; it's about bringing them back into the more healthy range (which hopefully some of our friends inhabit) that will work for the longer term.

Hence, there is an easy way to test our myths – ask other people. Surveys can seem daunting and can be hard to do if you do not feel you have many close friends. However, there are some useful tricks. You could, for example, ask your friends to survey their friends or you could post something on an anonymous answer-website.

A good survey questionnaire will be short, and will help you find out what standards other people are operating to. You can include several questions in your survey, but with today's social media you can easily ask one question at a time.

It can also be helpful to predict what people's answers might be – and then see what they actually are. Perfectionists tend to assume their perfectionist answers are justified. As in the example below, it may well be justified, but is it not normal?

Survey question	Expected answer	Actual answers
Do you take your smartphone on holiday so you can check emails?	Yes, but I only check it a couple of times a day.	
Your question:	Predicted answer:	
Your question:	Predicted answer:	

Christians have another whole level of myths and expectations associated with their faith, which (in human translation) can become filled with 'musts', 'oughts' and 'shoulds'. Complete the list below:

- I must go to both the morning and evening church services.
- I need to have a quiet time every morning for half an hour.
- A good Christian has read the whole Bible.
- The best Christians have secular experience before going into full-time Christian work.
- It's important to have Bible references for every situation.
- I have to confess every sin in detail, no matter how small it may be.

Your myth: _____

Your myth: _____

Martin Luther (1483–1546), the great Reformer, wrote, 'I tried to live according to the rule (of my monastic order) with all diligence . . . I confessed my sins . . . performed my allotted penance. And yet my conscience could never give me certainty.'[9] Luther's personal discovery of grace, and that God loved him anyway, transformed him completely. He still struggled with what theologians call 'scrupulosity', but he had a way of dealing with it:

> Sometimes it is necessary to drink a little more, play, joke . . . in defiance and contempt to the devil – in order not to give him the opportunity to make us scrupulous about small things. We will be overcome if we worry too much . . . What do you think is my reason for drinking wine undiluted, talking freely and eating more often – if it is not to torment and vex the devil who has made up his mind to torment and vex me![10]

I share Luther's belief that it can be good to tackle myths head on, and sometimes deliberately do things that challenge them to be shown for the shadows that they are. When we do this, it is important that we can sit with the uncomfortable feelings this push-back creates without seeing reassurance. This approach is often called 'Exposure and Response Prevention': we expose ourselves to the thing that makes us uncomfortable, and then refuse to respond to it until its sense of urgency and discomfort has passed us by.

Thoughtful goals

Let's spend a bit of time fathoming out some goals to set. It's helpful to be able to see how much you want to change – no-one is asking you to be a super-cool laid-back surfer dude, as that is probably not going to happen. Nor should it – God made you this way, but it just got out of calibration.

Please note, I did **not** say, be *clear* or *specific* about our goals. These are words that perfectionists latch onto, and it will take you forever to set any goals. However, a goal like: 'I want to be less of a perfectionist' is probably too broad. To help you, the table below has both general goals and specific examples. The space is limited, so you can't write too much!

General goal	Specific goal
Example: Become more relaxed about office etiquette.	*Stop washing up others' crockery and making comments on recycling and desk tidiness.*

Summary

At times when we cannot change our external world, we need to change our internal world. This is not about relaxing standards and being laid back; it is about seeing perfectionism for what it is and identifying the vicious circles that operate in our minds. We have now developed a more objective relationship with perfectionism and set some goals to work towards.

Exercises

1. Do you feel perpetually dissatisfied about your situation, but unable to make any changes?
2. 2. Do you fear mediocrity, criticism, uncertainty? Which do you fear most? How did this come about?
3. How does your faith fit in with your perfectionism? How has your expectation of God's action in your life become limited?
4. What was the biggest myth that you realized you had been believing? Was it helpful to see it labelled as a myth? How can you build on what you have learned?

5. CHANGING YOUR REALITY

Just doing as well as you did last time is not good enough.
(Michael Jackson, *Moonwalk*)[1]

Michael Jackson has sold about 750 million albums, with *Thriller* alone selling sixty-six million copies and leading the list of best-selling albums worldwide by a cool twenty-two million copies. Most people would argue that 'doing as well as you did last time' would be just fine, thank you. But the perfectionist is also the higher-and-higher-achiever who needs not just to maintain but to improve. The models in the last chapter showed how effort and striving are as important as results, and, if a result is achieved, the bar needs to be raised just to get the fix.

The sad story of Michael Jackson's life is that he went downhill and not uphill, retreating into his Neverland Ranch. He lost touch *with* reality – or maybe he could not bear to be *in* reality because of what it revealed about himself. The standards he set himself in *Moonwalk* (his only autobiography) were not being achieved, and with the breaking of the rules came the breaking of the man.

Instead of rules, which can break, this chapter will help you develop guidelines, which can encourage, direct and reassure.

But, most importantly, guidelines can bend. They are flexible friends who can get you out of trouble, but do not hold you to ransom.

Stress and strain

When I studied physics at school, we learned about the physical properties called 'stress' and 'strain'. I'll spare you the technical definitions, but stress is the pressure an object is put under and strain is the amount of deformation you see. A good example is an elastic band: when you stretch it, it gets longer quite easily. An iron bar, by contrast, requires a lot of stress (force) to see some strain (bend).

But there comes a time when too much stress is applied. Think of a plastic ruler. It bends quite easily with a bit of force, then takes more force to cause a larger bend, and then snaps, seemingly without warning. This breaking point is, of course, predictable and repeatable – it just seems to be a surprise. Other materials will bend and not return to their previous shape. Think of a coat-hanger which bends elastically with a small amount of force, but bends out of recognition if you really yank it.

We want you to be able to manage stress so that you stay in the 'strain' zone, and don't end up in the 'snap' or 'distorted' zones. The stress we are under is partly external (and less open to change), but partly internal, and this is where work can be done. Ask yourself: are your rules adding to your stress?

Stress → Strain → Snap?

The nice thing about physics is that it is based in reality. We can predict and experiment; we can find places to fail safely (like the first time you rode a bike); and we can even change the physical properties of our brains. Are you about to snap? Maybe this book can get you back into the strain zone, even if it can't reduce the stresses you are under.

Flexible friends

In 1974 Access™ Cards were like today's Visa™ Cards. Banks launched an advertising programme based on the idea of the card being your 'flexible friend'.[2] Sure, it could produce money from bank machines in distant countries, but that would not have been much good if it had snapped in your wallet when you sat on it in the plane. Access™ worked in the strain zone, and not the snap zone.

People usually snap because of rigid rules. To the perfectionist, anything short of perfection might seem like goal failure – even moral failure. This is because self-esteem depends on achievements and effort – remember the model of chapter 4? But snapping doesn't exactly help you get what you want either, as you start moving from being an 'achieving' perfectionist to being a 'failing' one.

Perfectionists are worried about changing their high standards, because they dislike the idea of lowering them. As a result, perhaps it is better to think about the opposite of rigidity, which is of course flexibility. Like Access™, you'll be able to manage the strain without snapping.

Instead of thinking about rules, which often leave us as hostages to fortune, it might be more helpful to think about guidelines. Rules break, but guidelines bend . . .

Guidelines can still be powerful motivators and helpful 'guides' to behaviour. Most dictionaries define a guideline as a principle, or something setting out a direction or course of action.

- In the table opposite, can you come up with a 'guideline' version of the rules on the left?
- Then write your own rules, and their guideline equivalents, in the last rows.

What makes a good guideline?

Some people might find this exercise a bit hard to fit to their rules, or that it doesn't really click with their way of thinking. Also, rules can sound a bit like guidelines, so we apologize if it seems like we are making an unhelpful division above, although it will help some people.

Instead, you might like to think of what the rule / guideline *feels* like. They will often look just the same to the casual observer. Can you tell who is a perfectionist or not by how hard they work?

The key question to ask is: **How do you feel when you remember your rule/guideline?**

Rule	Guideline
I must phone my wife every lunchtime from work, at about 12:45pm.	It helps my wife to hear my voice each day, as she sometimes only converses with the kids.
I have to eat fewer than 1,250 calories per day in order to maintain an acceptable figure.	It is good for me to have a healthy and balanced diet.
If I remember everyone's birthdays, then they will like me and notice my work.	
My house/desk/office must be tidy in order to improve my productivity and give others a good impression.	
I need to do something outstanding every day in order to make the most of my life.	
My rule:	My guideline:
My rule:	My guideline:

- If you feel encouraged and stimulated, and can manage at this pace, and no-one is getting hurt, then keep going.
- If you feel awful and under pressure, and others are starting to suffer around you, then something probably needs to change.

Embedding flexibility

Before you will truly trust your new flexible guidelines as your main motivators and principles, you need to 'break' the rules, before they break you. Our guess is that your head can see the value of guidelines over rules, but, if push came to shove, you would resort back to the old pattern. Better the devil you know . . .

Here are four experiments you can do to see the rules for what they are – fantasies that don't actually exist, and can never be lived up to and can be broken quite easily. Read them all and see which one might work best for you. Try this a number of times, to make sure you have really broken that rule.

1. *The Continuum*

For any rule and the assumption driving it, perfectionists think in terms of either/or – if they are not doing something 100%, then they are not doing it enough, and so it might as well be 0% and totally ineffective. However, if you were to keep a diary, you would see times when you did not keep this rule 100%, but neither did you drop to 0%. Also, there was not a clear relationship between the amount you kept the rule and the ensuing productivity.

- Rule: I must always be *very available* for everyone in my team (could also be church, family, etc.).
- Assumption: If I am not 100% available, then I will miss something big or let someone down.

The chart on the page opposite shows the benefits of a more flexible attitude to 'availability' for someone responsible for a big team.

Least available		
I was away on holiday when a big deal broke, but the team handled it really well. I had to tidy up a few things on my return. **Quite productive**	**Partly available** I was asked to do a big project by my boss but did check in on the team twice a day. They could see I was tied up. **Very productive**	**Very available** I thought something was up so I cancelled a trip away. I didn't get much done in the office, got on everyone's nerves and nothing happened. **Unproductive**

On a blank piece of paper, mark out a continuum for your rule, from 100% observed to 0% observed. Think of some examples where you did not keep your rule 100%. If you can't think of any then keep a diary for a week to generate some. Reflect on each example. How productive were you? Is the relationship a straight line or not?

2. The Thought Experiment

The philosopher Robert Nozick describes this thought experiment in his book *Anarchy, State and Utopia*.[3] He asks us to imagine a machine that injects ecstasy-inducing drugs at just the right rate to cause the most amazing feelings. The machine can re-create the feeling of having won a tennis tournament, or having written a great poem, or being truly in love. However, of course, none of these things is actually happening. You haven't played tennis, there is no poem, and you are sad and alone.

The question is this: would you actually *choose* to be hooked into the machine for the rest of your life, with ecstatic emotions but no true experience? Most people say they would not like this, and would rather take their chances.

Extend this to the life of the perfectionist. Much of their 'drug' is what might one day happen if only they could work hard enough and long enough . . . They are not actually living the dream, and haven't achieved that much yet, but everything is blocked out by the dream of the fantasy life. Are you choosing the machine by accident? Do you really want to live this way?

Write out your reflections on this thought experiment here:

3. The Ball Dropper

The life of the perfectionist is a balancing act. Think of that circus act where someone spins plates on top of sticks. Each plate needs attention in turn, and at some point there will be too many plates – and the whole lot will come tumbling down. Maybe you went to a better circus than me, where the performer managed to take them down in a controlled manner – but most perfectionists don't have lives like that.

Imagine you are currently spinning ten or so plates, and you've noticed it is all getting a bit wobbly. Maybe that is why you are reading this book. There are two things you can now do: remove a plate, or take some of the wobble out of the ones that need to remain. Here is an illustration of each from my (Rob's) life as an over-achiever.

Removing a plate:

I used to row competitively. It was my main thing at university. I won the boat race for Cambridge and a gold medal at the World Student Championships. I was also studying medicine and had missed a fair bit of my course. It was four years until the next big target (the Sydney Olympics in 2000) and I needed to choose between rowing and medicine. However, it was also my main area of Christian ministry – sharing my faith with my sporting colleagues.

In the end I chose medicine, in part because to choose sport would have meant going full-time and dropping out of medicine, but also because God seemed to be telling me that that season was coming to an end. In medicine I found a new love in psychiatry, and this eventually led to starting up the Mind and Soul Foundation and writing books like this one.

From time to time I am tempted to restart serious sport. I miss the fun of the team and the buzz of winning. But whenever I get into a boat for more than one row, my back starts to hurt, and God reminds me of his guidance and my choice.

Removing some wobble:

The smart reader will have noticed that in the example above, I replaced the plate of sport with the plate of mental health ministry! I am a perfectionist after all. None of my current plates can be dropped, so I need to make sure I am not making them too big and hard to spin.

I do this by deliberately performing from time to time below what I can achieve. I don't get involved in some email conversations; I turn down speaking engagements; I keep several free evenings each week. Occasionally, I need to do more. I have let people down because someone in the family was ill, for example, but rather than agonize over it, I deliberately think of it as a way to recalibrate that plate.

I try not to be obviously rude (sorry if I have turned down your invitation!), but I would rather be rude than a perfectionist who has lost their discernment and perspective.

- Can you label some of the plates that are spinning in your life?
- What were your thoughts on reading the above?
- Are there any plates that you think you need to put down?
- What can you do to drop some balls gently, before your rules break you completely?

Notes:

The problem with procrastination

Procrastination is a good indicator of both your current level of stress and level of busyness and perfectionism. Michael Hyatt,[4] former CEO of the publisher Thomas Nelson, wrote, 'Perfectionism is the mother of procrastination.' When things are at the right level, life will be busy but enjoyable, but when you take on too much, one of the first things to appear is a tendency to procrastinate, hesitate or bail out.

Sky Sports News presenter, author and endurance athlete Julia Immonen says, 'Procrastination used to be my middle name because I was absolutely terrified of trying and failing. Now I would much rather try and fail than just be stuck in the same place. Adventure has been born in me, and I feel that nothing is impossible.'[5]

People procrastinate for a number of reasons, but the most common one is to delay starting a task out of a fear of doing it less than perfectly. We typically think that inaction is better than failure because failure is so loaded with challenge to our identities, but in reality of course, trying and failing is a lot more 'worthy' than just not giving it a go.

Writing a book is a helpful challenge to procrastination. Your publisher has given you a deadline, and paid you money to meet it. You hand something over to them, and it comes back in a glossy cover. And people can buy it in the shops. Any minute now, someone is going to see it for the twaddle it actually is . . .

Of course, this is one reason why some potentially great authors never hand anything in!

For Christians, this fear can be displaced onto God. Research among some college students found that people with obsessive-compulsive tendencies preferred to pray vague prayers like: 'God, please let things be better' than specific prayers about difficult situations.[6] They feared that if the prayers were not answered, then this was their fault for not praying in exactly the right way. Dennis Gibson writes,

> 'Seeking God's Will', 'The leading of the Lord', 'God is able'. These words readily degenerate into clichés that justify indecision. It is easier to say we are 'waiting on the Lord' than to do the hard work of making a decision . . . We 'put out the fleece' instead of using our best judgement, deciding, and learning from any painful consequences that ensue. We resist trial and error learning, which happens to be one of God's favourite ways to teach us wisdom.[7]

In which areas of your life do you procrastinate? Can you identify with some of the statements below? Did you notice that there is a link between procrastination and perfectionism? The longer you put something off, the more it pushes your perfectionism buttons and the more your rules 'must' be adhered to, so the more likely you are to put it off.

- A null mark for not handing in an essay is better than a grade D for poor work.
- A rushed essay started the night before a deadline can be of poor quality because it was rushed rather than because it was bad.
- Better never to date someone that make a complete fool of yourself.
- Better to change at the last minute and then dash out to a party than to spend time choosing from outfits that you feel all make you look fat.

- Better not to do your music practice between lessons, so when you play a wrong note it can be blamed on that.
- Writers'/painters'/actors' block – better to be between jobs than to put on a poor show.

It is beyond the scope of this book to deal with all the various forms of procrastination, but it is something that can be overcome. You will find some steps to follow as outlined below, but if procrastination is a major problem for you, we would recommend section 7.8 of *Overcoming Perfectionism* (see Appendix 2).

1. Monitor your emotions while procrastinating. Is it really making you forget all about the problem? The deadline is not till next week, but how are you feeling just now?
2. See your worst-case scenario for what it is – usually the result of catastrophic thinking. When you write it down on paper, you can usually see that it is indeed an extreme statement and come up with a more balanced one.
3. Make predictions about how not procrastinating will go, and then test them out and see what happens. Do an experiment to see what the reality is.
4. Chunking. How do you eat an elephant (as the old adage goes)? The answer is: one bit at a time. Breaking down tasks can make them seem more manageable, and you get a small reward each time you complete a stage.
5. 'Just do it' is the Nike™ school of thought in dealing with procrastination. Once you have cracked procrastination a couple of times, many future opportunities to faff can be overcome by simple reminders to 'just do it'!

	Worst-case scenario	Experiment	Chunking	Just do it
What perfectionists do	Extreme: If I hand in a poor report, everyone will think I am a complete idiot.	Prediction: I hand in my report and am summoned before the managing director.	Writing a book on perfectionism is impossible – it will always be imperfect.	Procrastination seems like a friend – it will keep on popping up to offer denial and promises of peace.
*A **better** way*	Balanced: My report is not brilliant, but I have written good ones on average.	Reality: I handed in a few pages and called it a draft. Everyone was fine, and I got an extension and even some tips.	We wrote this book one chapter at a time, and that was after some planning stages and before some editing stages.	A big 'Just do it' post-it note on your computer can help with 75% of procrastination cases! What would work for you?

G. K. Chesterton once said, 'If a job is worth doing, it is worth doing badly!'[8] What he meant by this was that you have actually put a lot of effort into that essay/project/gift, and even if you have run out of time and it is not finished to your perfectionist standards, it has still been worth the time and effort. It will also be well received, with gratitude and thanks.

The table on the previous page summarizes the hidden elements of procrastination and contrasts them with a more constructive way to think and behave.

Summary

At times when we cannot change our external world, we need to change our internal world. This is not about relaxing standards and being laid back, but about seeing perfectionism for what it is and identifying the vicious circles that operate. We have developed a love-hate relationship with perfectionism and set some goals to work towards. We have addressed the issue of procrastination, identifying it as a clear and negative outworking of our perfectionism. We have offered a few strategies to overcome it.

Exercises

1. How much of each week do you spend in the stress zone and how much in the snap zone?
2. What do you think of the idea of flexibility? Is it a weakness or a strength? Are guidelines better helps to living than rules?
3. What are your most troublesome rules? What alternative guideline did you come up with?

4. Which of these four techniques did you find most helpful, and why? (The Continuum, The Thought Experiment and The Ball Dropper.)
5. How do you procrastinate? Were you able to influence one area of your life in which you do? What did this feel like?

6. ACHIEVING EXCELLENCE

Christianity is both the easiest and the hardest religion.
We need only come with empty hands, and then learn to
sit on them.

(Attributed to Francis Schaeffer)

The thing that marks Christianity out from other religions is the idea of grace. This beautiful doctrine is what saves us and sanctifies us, for it is Jesus who has made it all possible, not us. Many Christian books on busyness and perfectionism ask people to 'rest' in this grace, and this is usually about doing less. But we have already discussed that for some people, doing less is not an option, and for others, doing things is what they think God put them on this earth for . . .

A better skill to *learn* might be to discern when it is right to rest and right to act – to come with empty hands and to sit on them, as the quote above reminds us. A key skill for any perfectionist to learn is when to work hard, and when to turn off the drive and have fun. The phrase 'work hard, play hard' is used by perfectionists who have realized they need to do something like this, but haven't really fathomed it out.

A related skill to *learn* is how to do both – to work hard *and* have fun at the same time. Eric Liddell, the runner in the film *Chariots of Fire*, said, 'When I run, I feel His (God's) pleasure.' Liddell had learned the art of running fast *and* resting in grace at the same time. We believe that both these skills are things you can *learn*, with proven techniques and practice. And this is what the rest of this book is about.

Called or driven

There is one sure-fire way to make a mess of your life as a perfectionist, and that is to be driven by the wrong thing. Proving your parents wrong, desperately avoiding failure, seeking popularity for popularity's sake . . . these toxic motivations will always send you down the wrong road. Author Brené Brown said, 'When perfectionism is driving us, shame is riding shotgun, and fear is that annoying backseat driver.'

Yet we are called to do things. American pastor and author John Piper has said, 'God is most glorified in us when we are most satisfied in him.'[1] To many people, this means we need to spend time in prayer and contemplation and Bible study – but what if this satisfaction also comes in the midst of everyday life, or when using our talents?

To put it another way, we are most ourselves when we find ourselves in relationship with God and doing the 'good works, which God prepared beforehand' for us to do (Ephesians 2:10). Again, these 'good works' are traditionally seen as evangelism, service, even paid Christian ministry, but what if it was the case that they were, instead, living the life that God has given us, he has equipped us for, has made us good at? I (Rob) am a psychiatrist. Should I give that up and only write books like this one?

I hope you are all saying 'No!' at this point. I hope you feel deep down that there is something holy in what I do, maybe even in the health services that God has blessed us with. I feel as 'called' to do what I do as much as Will feels called to full-time Christian ministry. Both of us need to make sure that we do not become 'driven'. My Christian identity and my expressed identity need to flow from the same place. I *am* a Christian psychiatrist – a psychiatrist who is a Christian, and a Christian who is a psychiatrist.

> For Christians, there are only two kinds of achievers in this world—those who are called and those who are driven. The task for Christian achievers is to discern their true vocation so that they can live in sync with the divinely-designed inner rhythm of their souls.
> (Ashley Null)[2,3]

The quote above is from one of my mentors who is a lead chaplain for the Olympic Games. Every four years he counsels amazing athletes who have not understood this. Many are gold medal winners. But what do you say to the man or woman who has won an Olympic medal, except to have another go in four years' time? Ashley says that instead of finding their calling, 'many strive to use all their God-given gifts and abilities to create an identity completely independent from him. Cut off from the sense of wholeness that comes from God's unconditional love for them, they are forced to produce their own worth.'[4]

Bad sports psychology tries to harness this inner neediness as the drive to excel, to beat, to conquer, to stamp on the opposition. This is not confined to sport – many banks actively recruit people with insecurities and shallow ambition, as they know this produces work-horses to build the bottom line.

As a result, excellence and achievement have got themselves bad names in many Christian circles as the places where Mammon rules at the expense of worship and faith. And it goes both ways. Coaches worry that spirituality and religion will dampen the athlete's zeal to win. Clergy worry that this member of their flock is trying to serve two masters, and they ask them to choose.

> Billy Sunday was a professional baseball player from 1883 to 1892, when he gave it up to enter full-time Christian ministry. He listed[5] a number of reasons why he had left sport behind: because 'it develops a spirit of jealousy, it simply amuses mankind rather than serving them, morality is not essential to success, and I felt called of God to do his service' (and so on).
>
> In keeping with the growing fundamentalist movement of his era, Sunday believed that Christian holiness required complete separation from the wicked ways of the world.

Theologically, Billy Sunday committed an error: he believed that the *venue* of his life set the temperature for his spiritual life. But, to use some theological terms, sin is 'ontological' rather than 'systemic' – that is to say, it is part of our human nature and not bound up with any particular system or culture or job.

Reintegrating work and faith

Because we believe your faith plays such a fundamental role in helping you recover from perfectionism, it is essential for you to gain a strong sense of integration between your faith life and your working life. Compartmentalizing your faith and work will leave you 'performing' in each sphere, whereas integration undoes your pretence and invites authenticity into both areas. Ultimately, we need a Saviour, not a lifestyle.

> The logical answer of the radical seems to be that sin abounds in culture, that Christians [need to] have passed out of darkness into light, and that a fundamental reason for separation from the world is the preservation of the holy community from corruption.
> (Richard Neibuhr)[6]

The reality is that many people merely relocate their painful inner baggage from secular to spiritual locations, and not much changes. How much better it would be to deal with the issues *in situ*, where Jesus will meet with them. Their issues do not arise from the sport (business/achievement) itself, but the motivation behind why their accolades are being sought. Changing the venue or the goal of our activity will never provide an answer to the problems of our hearts.

Set against Billy Sunday's approach are the examples of Eric Liddell and his modern followers in all walks of life. Such people believe that the Christian life for them *is* one of excellence and using their God-given talents. Martin Luther said that every sphere of life was profitable as a Christian, as a 'hidden instrument of God's sustaining work of human society'.[7] Excellence is truly available to us when we live within the boundaries of God's gifting and calling for our lives.

There is one important consideration here. Luther was quite clear[8] that in order for secular vocations to rank alongside spiritual ones, they must offer some kind of service to human society. In sport we see the solidarity of the fan base, the healthy expression of competition, and the role of older athletes as models for the young. There are equivalents in other fields of achievement too: Channel 4's programme *Secret Millionaire* is one such example,[9] where unknown business people get the chance to fund local projects and see the look in people's eyes when they spring the surprise.

Reflection

- What benefits can you think of?
- Do they outweigh the problems of perfectionism?
- To ask the question another way, can these achievements be 'holy' achievements?

Notes:

Transforming hearts

Taking this further, for perfectionists, these arenas of success can be the very places where they work out their spiritual lives. They are sinners and God is there to save; they are foolish, and God is wise; they are 'a mist' (James 4:14), and God is everlasting. If knees can be bended in church, then they can also be bended (and bended before Christ) on the racetrack, in the boardroom and on the trading floor. As Ashley Null says, 'In the hard-bitten arena of professional sports, Christian athletes learn daily what it means to be called and not driven.'[10] Others can too.

> I (Rob) am not about to give up being a psychiatrist – as far as I know! This means I will be spending over forty hours a week in this role. This is going to have an impact on my spirituality, either good or bad. Will I indulge my natural bias to perfectionism and find my identity away from God? Or will I use these hours to get to know him better, to put others first, to practise fairness and openness, to speak up for those who have no voices? I can learn to be called and not driven, but mainly through self-effacement and putting others first.
>
> One of my other mentors, Dr Nick Land, has written about this style of medical leadership and how to acquire it.[11] He says, 'We are called to be salt and light. Some Christians argue that as "strangers in a foreign land", we should avoid involvement in secular structures. But Jeremiah, writing to the people of God in exile, instructs them to work for the peace and prosperity of the city in which God placed them.'

Transforming cultures

Yet again, what if it was about more than just the individual? What if it was about actually changing the *culture* of perfectionism? If people can grow in the assurance of their calling, they can be increasingly free to live with the nature God intended them to have from the beginning.

This joy[12] is the result of using their talents without fear of failure, in the full knowledge that this was why they were born. It's fun and pure and real – even holy. And it is infectious.

The athletes and those around them (and here we can substitute businessmen, academics, community workers, you name it) are grateful and able to express visibly their gratitude for:

- Jesus' saving grace that made them alive again
- their physical gifts that gave them a venue in which to work this all out
- the struggles and successes that come as part of God's plan.[13]

St Paul, in Philippians 3:1–10, echoes this. He was the consummate over-achiever, yet he boiled it all down to v10: 'that I may know him and the power of his resurrection, and may share his sufferings'.

When Christian achievers, in sport and also other areas, can be clear about who they are and why they do what they do and what it means to them, this is natural evangelism.

Questions

- Would you play sport on a Sunday? Or work on a Sunday? Reflect on this – why / why not?
- Do you feel called or driven, or a bit of both?
- Thinking about the calling, how does your area of achievement serve society?

- Thinking about your drivenness, have you considered asking God to bring healing to some of the areas where you feel compelled to perform?
- Have you considered speaking about your faith to your colleagues/team mates? Could you pray for the courage and opportunity to take a step forward with this?

A sabbath rest

One of the principles of the Christian life is the sabbath: that God laboured for six days creating the world and then rested on the seventh. This has been traditionally interpreted as not working on the sabbath, with some Jewish traditions giving this a very strict interpretation. It was the start of the idea of a weekend, and has persisted despite an attempt during the French Revolution to make a week ten days long!

But what does sabbath mean to the perfectionist who is not good at stopping? I know several people who refuse to darken the doors of a church because they think sitting in rows is passive and not for them (not that that is what we necessarily do anyway). They also struggle with the idea of going on holiday, unless it involves extreme sports. One sports holiday company, Neilson,[14] have as their slogan: 'Relax as hard as you like.'

> My (Will's) natural disposition to activity has made resting very hard indeed. My wife often laughs about my inability to sit still on our honeymoon. She recounts how, wanting to relax on her sun lounger with a nice book, she would send me off on errands and tasks around the small island: one hour of snorkelling, one hour collecting shells, one hour watercolour painting, sixty press-ups, a canoe trip . . . and so it went on.

> I have realized that I am wired in a particular way. I
> can become perfectionistic in the activity I am doing, but
> I can also become perfectionistic about the sort of 'rest' I
> should be doing too. I have learned that it is my attitude
> towards an activity that can make it restful. As a result, when
> I want to rest, I tend to go running or do press-ups! Equally, I
> have given up trying to pray in a quiet room on my own. My
> prayer life has taken off on my bicycle commute, my river
> runs and, most importantly, while fishing.

Some of my (Rob's) most treasured books on theology[15] do
not have sabbath listed in their indexes. The Old Testament
gives many instructions about what should and should not be
done on the sabbath day. But the New Testament interprets
this in a number of ways:

- Mark 2:27 says, 'The Sabbath was made for man,
  not man for the Sabbath.' Jesus was critiquing those
  who had made the sabbath a book of rules for their
  own advancement. I can think of those who, as we
  discussed in the previous section, have made the
  Christian walk overly spiritual – and for their own
  ends. See Luke 6:9, John 9:14, and many other
  scriptures also.
- Colossians 2:16 says, 'Let no one pass judgment on
  you . . . with regard to a festival . . . or a Sabbath.'
  Again, the criticism is against those who would 'puff up'
  super-spiritual notions of a sabbath for their own false
  humility (v. 18) with the 'appearance' of wisdom
  (v. 23a). Interestingly, the writer goes on to say (v. 23b)
  that such regulations lack any value in restraining
  sensual indulgence. The perfectionist knows all too
  well the limitations of rules.

- Hebrews 4:8–10 describe the sabbath rest as something clearly in the future, perhaps because the intended readers of that book were resting up rather too much. But the *Message* translation says this: 'At the end of the journey, we shall surely rest with God.'

The evidence for a rigid Sunday rest is lacking in the Bible. There is a clear pattern set down in the Old Testament of work and the enjoyment of that work, and the one-in-seven principle is not a bad guide, but it is equally clear that avoiding all effort on a Sunday, or limiting your efforts to only religious ones, is a man-made rule – of limited value and open to human abuse. What is key here is the spiritual value of 'sabbath rest' that we make a priority within the rhythms of our unique working lives. Christian rest expert Shelly Millar argues, 'A rhythm of rest is a state of being, not something we do.'[16]

Rest (without the rigidity) is particularly important for those of us with a leaning towards perfectionism. Millar again says, 'Without Sabbath, it is easier to fall into people pleasing and making decisions based on selfish motives, not only in volunteerism and ministry vocation, but also in core relationships.'

Some people, like Eric Liddell, have made decisions such as not competing on Sundays, but for those in most arenas of modern sport and many workplaces, this is often not possible. Sabbath rest is essential, but it can come in all sorts of forms and times. The key to success here is seeking God's plan for your rest, knowing that it is precious time with him and will always be good for you.

Champion golfer and Masters winner Bubba Watson is leading in a sport that is dependent on Sunday play and yet he has found his 'Sabbath rest' in other places. Watson has benefited hugely from the PGA Tour's weekly Bible study, held every Wednesday night during tournament weeks. He says, 'For me it's a way to get back [to being] connected with the Bible and with God and Jesus . . . Now you know other people you can talk to, ask questions to, tell them what you're thinking, tell them what's going on in your life.'

Bubba has avoided the trap of disconnecting his sport from his faith and instead uses it as a means of worship and outreach. He says, '[I am] realizing that golf is just an avenue for Jesus to use me to reach as many people as I can.'

Bubba also enjoys fellowship with members of his team, including his caddie Ted Scott. They ensure that God is a central part of the whole experience of professional sport.[17]

When to 'retire'

Sometimes rest is forced upon us. I have a preacher friend who jokes that God uses sporting injuries to speak to him. After tearing his cruciate, he had to spend a month in plaster and sitting down. His sermons from this time were amazing! I suggested that it might be easier for him if God didn't have to shout so loudly next time.

For most perfectionists, there comes a time when the achievement stops. Athletes have to retire from competitive sport. Business people (even those who own their own companies) have to stand aside for the next generation of directors. Church leaders have to make sure they are growing young leaders, and this means that one day one of them will lead instead.

The challenge here is to move on well. I don't use the word 'retirement', because that is not found in the Bible. It saddens me when people get to sixty-five and retire from life as well as from work. Given that there will be a transition at some point in the future, here are some questions to ask yourself in preparation:

- Do you have good people around you who can tell you when it is time to stop doing something? Without them, how will you know?
- Is God calling you into something new? Perfectionists never retire anyway; they usually move on to something new. But is this a calling or a drivenness and a need to be busy?
- How are you preparing to finish well? Management guru Peter Drucker is alleged to have said, 'There is no success without succession.' Are you planning your replacement now?
- If your self-esteem is tied up in your success, then how will you avoid depression when you retire? It is unlikely that you will be as good at something else . . .

Notes:

> When I (Rob) decided to retire from competitive rowing, I had to ask myself some hard questions about self-esteem. I could have stayed involved on the edges of the sport, perhaps coaching a bit. But I was worried about turning into a bore, telling stories about the good old days. The older you get, the better you were!

> I could also have thrown myself into another sport. I was doing a reasonable amount of road cycling at the time. This was a good choice, because I am the wrong build for a cyclist and was never in any danger of winning the Tour de France. I was average at cycling – I had to look to God for my identity. Even now I am still cautious about getting involved in a lot of sport. I am happy to be in shape, but don't want to be consumed by the need to do so.

Summary

We can rest up when we have 'fought the good fight . . . finished the race [and] kept the faith' (2 Timothy 4:7). But for now we need to make sure we are called and not driven, which requires us to integrate our work and worship – indeed the Hebrew word *avodah* can mean both work and worship. In the next chapters we shall learn the attributes of gratitude and self-compassion which will aid this integration.

Exercises

1. How good are you at knowing when to do less and when to do more? How vulnerable are you to people asking you to do things – can you say 'no'?
2. How good are you at taking a holiday / dealing with sickness or injury? What does the word 'sabbath' mean to you?
3. Have you thought about retirement? What plans have you made so it will not be a massive shock or a reflex leap to something else?

7. PRACTISING GRATITUDE

If the only prayer you said was thank you, that would be enough.

(Meister Eckhart)[1]

If we harness our deepest vulnerabilities to the express-train of perfectionistic activity, two things happen:

- We feel like we are making things better.
- We are distracted from our own heartache.

Of course, once the activity fix has been achieved, reality breaks through, and, plagued by dissatisfaction, we look for the next round of activity to escape through.

For a while I (Will) was hooked by one of the relocation housing shows. Typically, they displayed England on a dreary November day, rain pouring down, and a garbage truck ploughing through puddles of water alongside a pavement strewn with rubbish. By contrast, they showed Sydney, Australia, bathed in sunshine with people roller-blading to work alongside the golden sands of Bondi Beach. Dissatisfaction naturally fuels aspiration.

My love of this sort of programme died around the same time that broadcasters started airing new shows called something like *Revisiting Relocation*. Epitomized by miserable English people cooking on BBQs in the Australian sun, these shows killed the dream that you could relocate from your tendency to dissatisfaction.

Perfectionism's greatest lie

Perfectionism's greatest lie is that 'if I just got this *one thing* sorted out, I would be happy/thankful/satisfied'.

St Augustine said that 'desire hath no rest, is infinite in itself, endless, and as one calls it, a perpetual rack, or horse-mill'.[2] By contrast, practising gratitude when your circumstances remain unresolved seems unnatural, because it is unnatural.

- Perfectionism says: Desire + Fulfilment = Happiness.
- Gratitude says: Desire + Fulfilment = Happiness is a formula that will have no bearing on your true happiness.

British psychologist Michael Eysenck developed the theory of the Hedonic Treadmill, which proposes that rather than happiness being a something we accumulate in greater measure, it is something that stays relatively stable in our lives regardless of our circumstances. On a treadmill you have to keep walking just to stay in the same place.[3]

Eysenck is one of many psychologists who have shown that far from it being an outlandish suggestion, people's happiness is relatively stable, and *circumstantial* changes have a very small impact on our happiness over the long term. One particular study found that a group of lottery winners and paraplegic victims of terrible accidents returned to their same general 'baseline of happiness' within a few years of the event.[4]

Of course, this is something that we all know is true. We read the papers and every day see unhappy successful people, depressed rich people, miserable famous people, yet we still believe the lie that material fulfilment will somehow release gratitude. Equally, I have spent times in HIV orphanages in Africa and been overwhelmed by the extreme joy, happiness and gratitude of some of the most deprived people on this planet.

Julia Immonen broke two Guinness World Records on her transatlantic row in 2011 / 12. She said,

> 'The moment you leave land behind, you are stripped of everything, all of your security is gone. As a result, you just feel so grateful for every little thing. After fifteen days at sea our automatic desalination pump broke, meaning we had to hand pump sea water for two hours to get just two litres of drinking water. That experienced totally changed me. I just felt that as long as I had that water, I had everything. I was so filled with gratitude, it put everything else into perspective.[5]

If we can agree that perfectionism is offering us a false road to fulfilment, we have made great progress on our journey through this book. Rob and I firmly believe that while material success cannot fundamentally change your experience of life, living in gratitude to God can do so. The way to change your happiness level (called Hedonic Adaptation if you want the technical term) is not to change your circumstances, but by changing your goals, values and interpretation of a situation.[6] Just like Julia and her water pump, it was a change of perspective and not a resolution of her difficult circumstances that brought her joy.

Gratitude: old wisdom recovered

Robert Emmons[7] is one of a number of notable psychologists who are taking an interest in the power of gratitude. He says, 'Gratitude is literally one of the few things that can measurably change people's lives.' Recent psychological research has shown that gratitude improves emotional and mental health, increases the experience of positive emotions and reduces destructive impulses.

In a culture that actively works to provoke your dissatisfaction, developing the muscle of gratitude could be your most powerful means of freedom from perfectionism. However, this is not a new revelation by modern psychologists, but an old piece of wisdom that permeates the whole of the Bible.

The instruction to 'give thanks' occurs thirty-nine times in the New Testament. The Greek word *eucharisteo is* a combination of *eu* (good) and *charis* (grace). Within the Gospels Jesus 'gives thanks' at many key points in his ministry, including the raising of Lazarus (John 11:41), the Last Supper (Luke 22:17) and the feeding of the five thousand (Luke 9:16). It is from this word that we have derived the word for the Holy Communion: the Eucharist, at which we celebrate God's *charis* (grace) to us in the sacrifice of Jesus for our sakes. Gratitude or 'worship' is at the centre of our created purpose, and yet it is often so elusive in our busy lives.

Building gratitude

It is good to think of 'building the muscle of gratitude', since this is an active process and not a reactive event. Sadly, when it comes to thankfulness, the dominant approach in society (and often the church) is conditional: I will be thankful when . . .

- I am asked to become a partner in the firm
- I get in shape (that elusive six-pack)
- I get well/healed/an operation date
- I get married/have children
- I get my prayers answered.

Western, twenty-first-century thankfulness can nearly always be prefaced with 'I'. If we allow this to remain the case, then we shall continue to spin round a vicious cycle:

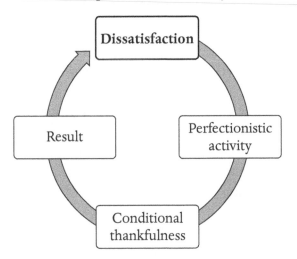

Biblical gratitude is *not* conditional upon positive circumstances, but is an attitude of heart that exists regardless of either life's ease or life's hardship. Our (Will's) family verse is framed above the loo: 'I have come that you may have life – life in all its fullness' (John 10:10, Good News Translation). I have referenced this verse in countless talks and sermons, seen it emblazoned on stickers and in memes, and heard it ringing throughout many hymns.

What I came to realize after many years was that I was reading something else. I was reading what I hoped it would say: 'I have come that you may have life – life in all its *softness*.'

My disaffection with God grew when life was hard; my thankfulness was dependent upon things working out as planned. This verse is not offering me half of life: it is offering me 'fullness' which is all of life's 'softness and hardness' together. It is Jesus' presence in the fullness of life that makes it good, not the circumstances themselves. We need to keep coming back to this fact.

Paul's gratitude secret

> I rejoiced in the Lord greatly that now at length you have revived your concern for me. You were indeed concerned for me, but you had no opportunity. Not that I am speaking of being in need, for I have learned in whatever situation I am to be content. I know how to be brought low, and I know how to abound. In any and every circumstance, I have learned the secret of facing plenty and hunger, abundance and need. I can do all things through him who strengthens me.
> (Philippians 4:10–13)

Paul's experience is very much one of the 'fullness' of life, from shipwreck and prison to God encounters and growing churches. He is not unmoved by the concern of the Philippian church, but equally he is not dependent upon it. The Greek word for 'content' is *autoarkas*, literally meaning 'independent'. This is not a denial of his actual circumstances, neither is it a Bear Grylls survival technique: it is a refusal to allow his circumstances to dictate his spiritual status as a worshipper. Paul's gratitude to Christ is unmoved by famine or feast.

Strength in adversity
Both Rob and I really enjoy exercise and, to support our various sporting pursuits, we have needed to strengthen

our muscles. This typically takes the form of what is called 'resistance training' – the sort of training that actually hurts quite a lot, but the discomfort is worth it for the reward of riding the wave or making your boat move quickly through the water.

Gratitude is a muscle that is also strengthened through resistance training. When things are going wrong and we practise gratitude *anyway*, we are disconnecting our disposition from our circumstances. Just like lifting weights, the more we lift, the stronger we become and the more we can lift. The more we practise gratitude in difficult circumstances, the more grateful we become and the more able we are to practise gratitude when things are tough. Paul describes gratitude within adversity in Romans 5:3–5 (*Message* version):

> We continue to shout our praise even when we're hemmed
> in with troubles, because we know how troubles can develop
> passionate patience in us, and how that patience in turn forges
> the tempered steel of virtue, keeping us alert for whatever
> God will do next.

Exercise: Mining gratitude
Bring to mind a situation that was difficult for you or when you felt the outcomes were very dissatisfactory. Remind yourself of your feelings of deflation, frustration or disappointment.

Situation:

Now start to mine the situation for things that you could be thankful for. It doesn't matter how small they may be. Try to be attentive to the process, potential and people, not just the outcome of the situation. It may help you to write your findings down as a list. Like any mine, you can keep on going back to see if you find a bit more – so, do it for a few days in a row.

Notes:

Exercise: Thanks for time

One of the great sufferings of the perfectionist is the ticking clock. I wonder how long you spent on that last exercise? Five minutes, two minutes or thirty seconds? Did you even do it, or was it just about finishing the book? The urgency to complete the task list, to get the key to unlocking the problem, to achieving the goal, is always great, because for the perfectionist, time is always pressing.

One way to deal with this ticking clock is to turn up early for things. The same amount of tasks get done, but you are less worried about being late. However, some people will have started arriving early and found fifteen minutes to 'nibble' through a few emails on their smartphone.

In the 1930s the economist John Maynard Keynes predicted we would be working fifteen-hour weeks by 2030 because our technology would be so developed. Today we have time-saving technology far beyond Keynes' wildest imagination, but we are working seventy hours in the office and another twenty on our mobile phones. Perfectionists do not see new technology as a means of getting more recreation time, but as a means of getting more out of time.

So, let's do something different and see what happens. Arrive early for something and, before you do anything else,

- spend a few breaths thanking God for arriving early and the extra time you have
- look around you and notice one new thing – a leaf, a line, laughter – and say 'thank you'
- if you must use your smartphone, make your first email/text a small 'thank you' to someone in your life.

Notes:

God, gratitude and rest

The Bible rings with a chorus of gratitude to God, and the Psalms are its songbook. Practising gratitude from a secular psychological perspective may be helpful, but it is nothing compared to the power of practising gratitude to God.

> The LORD is my strength and my shield;
>   in him my heart trusts, and I am helped;
> my heart exults,
>   and with my song I give thanks to him.
> (Psalm 28:7)

You might think that all this singing and leaping is a waste of time. Yet it is a waste in the same way as was the perfume that was poured out on Jesus in Mark 14:3. In verse 4 the socially orientated perfectionist says, 'Why this waste of perfume?' when what is actually happening is a lavish expression of gratitude to God. The greatest statement of our worship is our willingness to sacrifice the thing that is most precious to us. For this woman, it was her perfume, worth 'over 300 denarii' (which was a year's wages) and also essential for her job.

A perfectionist's greatest sacrifice is undoubtedly their time. Without it, they cannot chase the dream or attainment. Spending our time in gratitude is a rebellion against the myth that we are in control, and acceptance that God is in control. Gratitude re-orders our souls from disquiet to peace. As St Augustine said, 'My heart is restless until it finds its rest in thee.'[8] Without a destination for our gratitude, we remain restless, but when gratitude finds its orientation, we find the rest our souls have been longing for.

Psalm 91:1 (NIV) reads: 'Whoever dwells in the shelter of the Most High will rest in the shadow of the Almighty.' The

Hebrew word translated as 'dwell' is *yashab*, which has a more self-directed meaning as 'remain or settle'. The word for rest (*lewn*) is more commanding: 'cause to rest or lodge'.[9] The implication of this psalm is helpful to us in understanding the correlation between gratitude and rest. To paraphrase with my own emphasis, 'When we choose to settle into a place of gratitude to God, he *causes us to rest* in his safety.'

Exercise: Resting prayer

Pray the ancient Easter Orthodox prayer, 'Lord Jesus Christ, Son of God, have mercy on me, a sinner', out loud twenty-five times. Try to use your in-breath to say, 'Lord Jesus Christ, Son of God', and your out-breath to say, 'Have mercy on me, a sinner.' Take care not to rush, but to rest in the prayer, attentive to your heart's gratitude to God for Jesus.

In-breath	Out-breath
Lord Jesus Christ, Son of God	Have mercy on me, a sinner

Notes:

Noticing goodness

In my (Will's) role as a vicar in London, I spend a lot of time with some very busy people whose marriages are in difficulty. There is undoubtedly a correlation between 'time poverty' and marriage problems, and this is often manifested in the phrase I hear a lot: 'He/She just doesn't seem to notice me any more.' It isn't that one partner in a relationship is not seeing the other partner; it's that they have become inattentive to either their needs or their disposition. Over a long period of time this inattentiveness can have a catastrophic effect upon the relationship.

Restoring the attentiveness of a marriage partner to their spouse is like reconnecting an artery to the heart. Something that was dying suddenly springs back to life, and is full of wonderment and expectation.

The same is true where perfectionism and gratitude are concerned. When we reconnect the heart to gratitude, our relationship with time changes. Once our relationship with time has changed, we become attentive to ourselves, others and to God himself.

Exercise: Attentiveness

Decide that you are going to take three minutes for this exercise and try to use all of it. Set an alarm on your phone if that helps.

Take a close look at the palm of your hand. Explore the different colours and contours. Look closely at the folds and lines, and the track where they lead. Now turn your hand over and look at the different shades of skin, veins and tendons. Explore the way the palm and back of your hand meet, and how the skin changes. Now begin to flex the joints in your hand, and enjoy the dexterity and movement that is available to you.

Conclude your three minutes with a prayer of thanksgiving for your hands.

Following this exercise:

- What surprised you about being deliberate with your attention?
- What did you notice about your hand that was new?

- How activated was your sense of wonderment about your hands? What did you notice about your hand that was new?
- How activated was your sense of wonderment about your hands?
- How natural was your sense of gratitude to God?

Notes:

Connectedness and gratitude

God has given us the capacity for deep connectedness, and yet we often tend towards a life of limited focus and shallow attention. Many of the mantras of modern living seem to celebrate a fast-paced, low-commitment way of living fuelled by a FOMO (fear of missing out) anxiety. How many of these phrases have resonated with you?

- Never get bogged down in the detail.
- Live every day like it's your last.
- A change is as good as a rest.
- You have got one life, so live it.
- If you're not living on the edge, you are taking up too much space.
- Go for it now! The future is promised to no-one.
- To keep your balance, you must keep moving.

These and hundreds of quotes like them have been attributed to everyone from Seneca to Shakespeare and Woody Allen to Albert Einstein. They are a timeless tribute to the disquiet of the human heart and its reluctance to be truly connected. They are not worth the breath it takes to speak them!

Perfectionism thrives on an outlook that is narrow and shallow. Efficiency commands that the perfectionist limit their vision to only those things that may assist them in reaching their goal.

My (Will's) sat-nav is a perfectionist. He[10] instructs me on the fastest route to my destination, offering me the least scenic, least interesting journey. If I try to take a detour from his directed pathway, he tries to redirect me to the route that he had planned.

Just like a sat-nav, perfectionism leads us through narrow and shallow waters of human relationships. Think about the relational implications of the statements that began this section. Do they make for good dating advice? Would they be useful in family counselling or marriage work? Perfectionism is always in a hurry to get to its next destination, and as a result, it is in danger of commoditizing people as a means to 'get on'.

Notes:

Commoditizing or connected

Many years ago, I (Will) was invited by a dear friend to attend a grand media dinner. I was not in the media, and in fact I knew very little about the media at all. I dressed the part and took a seat at the beautifully decorated table with about thirty other people. Knowing just one person there was slightly daunting, not least because he was right at the other end of the table. I was pleased when an absolutely beautiful young woman came and sat down next to me. She was incredibly enthusiastic to tell me all about her role in the media, her experience and ambition for the future.

Having nearly finished the main course, she asked me, 'And what do you do in the media?' I am guessing that she had presumed I was a new hot-shot producer or something. So, when I told her, 'I am a school teacher', she could not hide her disdain. Falling abruptly silent, she completed her main course, picked up her chair and moved it to the space between two other guests, and proceeded to enjoy the rest of her meal there. I was left to eat my pudding in silence, not having got to know the guest on my right-hand side and now having a gaping two-foot space between me and the next person on my left.

I am thankful for that experience, because it usefully illuminated my own misuse of other people. I realized that the sense of shame and rejection I had felt was not dissimilar to the feelings that other people must have felt at my hands. My perfectionism draws my attention to the famous person I could network with, over the friend I know so well. My perfectionism wants to categorize people as 'strategic' and not as 'precious'. And yet all of this I must resist, because God has not created me for narrow and shallow relationships that serve my ambition, but for deep and connected ones that reflect the unique and precious identity of each person he has created.

Transforming relationships

When we apply the principle of practising gratitude to our relationships (old and new), life can quickly be transformed. In chapter 1 we introduced you to the other-orientated perfectionist, whose relationships were damaged by their harsh expectations of others and their tendency to see people as a means to achieve their own agendas. To an extent, every perfectionist (if not every person) does this. Being 'hard-hearted' is the opposite to gratitude, and so actively being grateful both internally and externally softens our hearts towards others and softens others' hearts towards us.

Shelly's relationship with Michael was not in a good place. He worked long hours running his own plumbing business, and their three young boys were very active and demanding. Shelly had very high expectations for herself, her home and her family. As a full-time homemaker, she prided herself on everything looking perfect. Michael often came home late, exhausted and dirty. It was the small things that enraged Shelly. She noticed how he kicked off his shoes in the hall, left his overalls on the floor, and generally made little effort. She always had a to-do list waiting for him that he seemed reluctant to respond to, and they quickly ended up rowing.

Shelly's attempts to practise gratitude towards Michael felt very unnatural at first. She was literally racking her brain to try to notice something that made her thankful, but over time her attentiveness paid off. She started to be generous with her time towards him, not rushing him along. She found that there was more and more about him that she liked, and amazingly, the more she noticed, the more he responded. His self-esteem seemed to grow through her gratitude. Instead of 'loafing around', he naturally stopped doing the things that Shelly had been complaining about. He even started to demonstrate gratitude to her for all of the things that she did to make their family happy.

Exercise

Bring to mind someone you know really well, maybe a parent, partner or friend. I'm sure a few annoying things pop into your mind. However, despite all of your familiarity, bring to mind as many things that you can be grateful for as possible. Now review your own feelings towards them. Are they strengthened or weakened? How will your reflection on them change your next encounter?

Notes:

Summary

Throughout this chapter, we have looked at the ways in which practising gratitude can transform your relationship with time, attention, rest and relationships. In preparation for our work on compassion in our final chapter, let's take a moment to reflect upon how gratitude affects your own view of yourself.

The reality for most perfectionists is that practising gratitude is hard because they have such a harsh internal narrative. Perfectionism, you could argue, is a misguided attempt to receive gratitude. That is why choosing to practise gratitude before you have received it makes so much sense. It breaks the faulty link between performance and affirmation.

You may well find that practising gratitude to God, and to others, is relatively straightforward. You may find success in being attentive to things in your circumstances or environment that you can be grateful for. But how about you? When it comes down to practising gratitude towards ourselves, can we hear the Master when he says, 'Well done, good and faithful servant' (Matthew 25:23)? That is when we know that our perfectionism is starting to heal.

Exercises

1. What have you learned about the power of gratitude to undo perfectionism?
2. What did you find most surprising about your initial attempts to use gratitude?
3. How was your relationship with time and rest affected by your new approach to gratitude?
4. Do you envisage a change in your relationships as a result of gratitude?
5. Could you incorporate a gratitude exercise like the hand observation one into your working day? How do you imagine this would influence your general experiences of life's stressors?
6. What do you find hard about being grateful towards yourself?

8. PRACTISING COMPASSION

*God's dream is that you and I and all of us realize that
we are family, that we are made for togetherness, for
goodness and for compassion.*[1]

(Archbishop Desmond Tutu)

A concert orchestra is made up of between seventy and a
hundred musicians. Each of them is highly competent and
has the potential to create beautiful music. However, they are
dependent upon the conductor to unify their musicality for
the common purpose of playing a symphony. Much like the
conductor of an orchestra, despite all of our potential, it is
our minds that provide the tone of our activity.

Think about all of the ways in which you could perform a
simple practical task like making a cup of tea for a colleague:
you could make it begrudgingly, graciously, spontaneously,
angrily, kindly – the list goes on. Playing an instrument or
making tea are practical activities, and yet the message they
give out is drastically affected by the tone that we apply to
them. Perfectionism is the conductor that has been setting the
tone of your life. However, he is not the only one equipped
for that role.

Neuroimaging shows us that habitual behaviour (positive or negative) can make our brain responses automatic: the same areas 'light up' in a person's brain because these are well-worn pathways of thinking. When people say things like: 'I can't help seeing things like that, it's just the way I am wired', they are right. It is the way they are currently wired, but it doesn't have to remain that way. We have neural plasticity: our brains can be rewired through practising mental exercises.[2] Now we are going to define compassion before looking at how compassion training can play a valuable part in overcoming perfectionism.

What is compassion?

Compassion is defined as 'the emotion one experiences when feeling concern for another's suffering, and desiring to enhance that individual's welfare'.[3] Psychologists describe it as having both an 'affective' (feelings) component and a 'pro-social' (active) component.

The Greek word for compassion, *splagchnizomai*, is only used in reference to Jesus in the New Testament. *Splagchnon* was Greek for 'spleen', and hence the inference was 'to be moved to your very guts', which were historically thought to be the seat of love and compassion. In the feeding of the five thousand story from Matthew 14:14 it says, 'When he went ashore he saw a great crowd, and he had compassion [affective] on them and healed [pro-social] their sick.'

This sort of compassionate activity was intended for all of Jesus' followers. In Luke 10:30–37 we read the ultimate parable of compassion: the good Samaritan. In this text the Samaritan man 'had compassion' (affective) for the beaten traveller. The 'pro-social' component was that he bandaged the man's wounds, put him on his own donkey and took him to an inn to be cared for. At the end of the passage, Jesus' instruction was (v. 37) to 'go, and do likewise'.

Jesus' attitude to compassion was not that it was the unique trait of kind people, or an automatic response to suffering, but that it was something that you could choose to be. And it appears that modern psychology and advanced neuroimaging techniques all agree with Jesus! Psychologist and compassion expert Helen Weng says, 'Compassion is a trainable skill rather than a stable trait.' Following a study at the University of Wisconsin, she reflected that 'after only seven hours of practice, people who trained in compassion behaved more generously compared to the other (control) group'.[4]

Why is compassion training helpful?

Throughout this book we have worked together to change your beliefs about perfectionism and your use of perfectionistic behaviours. However, without identifying a practical and opposing force to your perfectionistic impulses, you will always be vulnerable to relapsing into old habits.

Developing your ability to be more compassionate will in no way diminish your ability to achieve excellence in whichever sphere of life you are applying yourself. Remember that positive motivations are far more powerful than negative ones in the long term. Compassion training will enable you to move towards a much fuller and healthier way of living your life, and will help you develop far better social and interpersonal relationships.

If you think about the greatest commandment in Mark 12:30–31, it includes the instructions firstly, to love God and, secondly, to 'love your neighbour as yourself'. For perfectionists, this is very hard, since they very rarely have much love for themselves in the first place. As a result, they can find it very difficult to be compassionate to others, and find it especially hard not to fall into perfectionistic self-attacking thoughts and behaviours.

Practising compassion changes your self-approach, which over time can even change the structure of your brain. As one study concluded, '[This] training strengthened feelings of warmth and care toward oneself and others.'[5] The outworking of compassion training for Christian perfectionists could be something of a revolution in all areas of life, not least within their faith and spirituality.

What do I need to know before I start?

1. Practising compassion will not weaken my ability to achieve excellence.
2. Practising compassion will feel unnatural at first, but it will get easier over time.
3. My emotions are not 'dangerous' and can all be healthily engaged with.
4. Empathizing with others is a strength and not a weakness.
5. I will give myself time to practise compassion without rushing or bullying myself.

Compassionate attributes and skills

Compassion in this context is more than one simple emotion. It is a set of complex and interconnected motivations, reactions and responses. Psychologist Paul Gilbert[6] divides compassion into 'compassionate attributes' and 'compassionate skills'. The attributes form the framework through which you engage with the journey of life, and the skills are more conscious decisions that you make to deal with bumps in the road.

Below we have set out the key attributes and skills that we hope you will begin to develop. Please remember that this is just an outline of what we anticipate. It is not a tick list to complete within a certain time frame. In fact, be warned: it will take a while . . .

Compassionate attributes	Compassionate skills
Becoming more aware of our feelings and the feelings of those we come into contact with	Recalling your 'Compassion Home Base' (see below) when you are feeling vulnerable or self-attacking
Carrying the desire to be a blessing to others and ourselves, regardless of life's pressures	Bringing a balanced reflection to your situation when it appears catastrophic
Being able to sit with uncomfortable thoughts, memories and emotions without trying to escape	Listening reflectively to the feelings and opinions of others without defensiveness or shame
Becoming objective about the urgency we feel to achieve, fix, control or perform	Engaging in compassionate self-talk when in spirals of distress or pressure (self-soothing)
Living with a self-worth that comes from being a child of God	Looking outwardly to the needs of others and engaging in their plight with empathy

Exercise: Compassion for a friend

Find a comfortable and quiet place to sit for five minutes. Try to turn off any potential distractions. This exercise is just a reminder of what compassion looks like, and what feelings it evokes within us.

Bring to mind someone to whom you are very close. Spend some time simply remembering their good attributes and the connection that you feel to them. Try to avoid getting into too much detail, and gently redirect your mind to the task if it begins to wander.

Now try to recall an act of kindness or compassion that they have shown to you in the past. Spend some time exploring what was said and done, giving particular attention to the feelings that you experienced as a result of that incident. Try to notice if the memory affects your body in some way. Does it make you feel relaxed or warm? Do you smile in response to this memory?

When you feel you have explored it fully, pray for the person slowly and deliberately with the following prayer:

Dear Lord God,
I give you thanks for the relationship that I have with [name].
I remember fondly their good character and the gift of our
*   friendship.*
I am touched by their compassion for me.
I am reminded of your infinite compassion and love.
I pray that you might bless them with joy and peace at this moment.
In the name of your Son, Jesus Christ,
Amen

Following this exercise:

- Which different emotions did you experience during the exercise?
- How did your disposition change when you brought to mind the incident of compassion or kindness?
- Did any self-attacking or dismissive thoughts intrude in the exercise?
- If so, how did you manage them and continue to focus on the task?

- What did you notice about the way you prayed for the person in your reflection?
- Was it more compassion-filled than you expected?

Notes:

Compassion and the reward principle

When it comes to receiving compassion and kindness, people who struggle with perfectionism typically operate on a 'reward' basis. If you look back at the previous exercise, you will probably notice that you had no reservations about praying the compassion prayer for the individual who had shown compassion to you – they deserved the same reward.

For many perfectionists, the reward principle was established in childhood, where good behaviour equated to parental affection, but poor behaviour equated to parental rejection.[7] As a result, their emotional responses in adulthood follow the same pattern. We have seen this manifested in all areas of life, from business to the church, and even people's marriages, where physical affection is withdrawn if the partner is perceived to be 'undeserving'.

The reward principle is deeply flawed, for three main reasons:

1. It is highly subjective. What constitutes 'deserving behaviour' where loving kindness is concerned?
2. It is inhuman. It suggests that love is a response to goodness, not to personhood. If that were true, we would all be eternally lost.

3. It flows against grace. Jesus has specifically called us to love our enemies and bless those who persecute us.

If we return again to the Compassion Parable (Luke 10:30–37), you will notice several things about the reward principle. Jews and Samaritans were sworn enemies in the first century AD; the Jews treated Samaritans with disdain and even called them 'dogs'. The Samaritan man had compassion on the Jewish traveller despite this painful social discordance. The traveller had no means of rewarding the Samaritan for his kindness, not least because he had been robbed. The Samaritan paid for the man's ongoing care, with no conditions for repayment or even thanksgiving. Jesus was deliberately deconstructing the reward principle to demonstrate that true compassion was a gift of the giver, not a transaction with the recipient.

In order to make progress in practising compassion, we must decide to ditch the reward principle. Deciding that you will offer compassion to people regardless of whether they deserve it or not is foundational to overcoming perfectionism. This is a step further than simply disconnecting a person's value from their performance; this is an active decision to reward the undeserving.

Exercise: Compassion for the 'undeserving'

Find a comfortable and quiet place to sit for five minutes. Again, try to turn off any potential distractions.

Bring to mind someone who you have struggled to get along with, possibly at work or in the wider family. Once you have them in mind, scan your immediate emotional and physical disposition. Bring to mind a particularly difficult interaction with this person, and notice how your sense of injustice, defensiveness and frustration increases.

Now make a conscious decision to bless this person. Mentally list all of their positive attributes, no matter how small. Think about them in the context of their own family lives as children, siblings or parents. Imagine them in difficult circumstances requesting help or support.

Become aware of your own inner conflict between hostility and compassion. Be non-judgmental about this division. Actively allow it to exist, but make a decision to build your compassion regardless of how they may continue to respond to you.

Finally, slowly and deliberately pray this prayer:

Dear Lord God,
I give you thanks for the relationship that I have with [name].
I am mindful of their humanity and their positive attributes.
I resign my hostility and defensiveness about them to you.
I am reminded of your infinite compassion and love for me.
I pray that you might bless them with joy and peace at this moment.
In the name of your Son, Jesus Christ,
Amen

Following this exercise:

- Were you surprised by the strength of feeling that you held about the subject of this exercise?
- How uncomfortable did you feel when recalling a poor interaction with them?
- Did you notice any physical sensations or make any attempt to divert yourself from the subject?
- How difficult was it to decide to think compassionately about the subject?
- What impact did thinking about them in the context of their own family relationships make?

- Did the exercise make them more or less human?
  Did it make you more or less human?
- How did it feel to bless them actively in prayer?
- Could you create a list of other people to do this
  exercise about?

Notes:

Self-compassion

Thinking about compassion for someone we don't like very much brings us neatly on to ourselves. You may think I am joking, but in our experience the majority of people who struggle with perfectionism have a great battle to love or value themselves. That is not to say that they struggle to value what they do, but they simply don't value who they are. As you now know, this imbalance pushes people to do more while they feel less.

Self-compassion is really the litmus test of recovery for perfectionists. Christopher Germer writes, 'Self-compassion is simply giving the same kindness to ourselves that we would give to others.'[8] It sounds so simple, and yet most perfectionists would find the previous exercise much easier than the one to come.

> Having worked in the church for many years now, I (Will) know this to be true, both for myself and for many other leaders. Clergy typically spend hours and hours each week listening compassionately to the needs of others, and yet I have never met a more miserly bunch when it comes to

> self-care. 'When did you last have a day off?' is a standard
> clergy convention discussion point. Generally, the biggest
> number is celebrated with shocked applause, and anyone
> who has made it to the golf course in the last month looks
> at the floor in shame.

Self-compassion, however, should never be a subject of shame. It is a mind-set that facilitates the very essence of pastoral ministry. Self-compassion is imbibing the comfort of Jesus into our hearts, so that from that place of richness we might show compassion to a broken and hurting world. As Paul writes in 2 Corinthians 1:3–4, 'Blessed be the God and Father of our Lord Jesus Christ, the Father of mercies and God of all comfort, who comforts us in all our affliction, so that we may be able to comfort those who are in any affliction, with the comfort with which we ourselves are comforted by God.'

The three cords of self-compassion

We want to highlight three central 'cords' of Christian self-compassion, which work together to create a strong place from which God's compassion can flow in and out of your life. Ecclesiastes 4:12 says that 'a threefold cord is not quickly broken'.

Cord 1: Knowledge

In Philippians 1:9 Paul writes, 'And this is my prayer: that your love may abound more and more in *knowledge* and *depth of insight*' (NIV, emphasis added). Self-compassion is greatly strengthened by the understanding, for example, what you have developed through reading this book and participating in the various exercises.

- To lack knowledge is to remain enslaved to the automatic thoughts, feeling and responses of the past.
- Insight is the ability to apply the knowledge you have gained to particular circumstances, and so these two attributes (knowledge and depth of insight) make a powerful combination.

It is our hope that in future stressful circumstances you may be able quickly to identify old perfectionistic thoughts and behaviours, and offer yourself a truthful appraisal of their origin and value to you. Equally, having confidence in the power of compassion and gratitude, you may choose to employ a new approach to your circumstances: one originating from healthy, biblical self-esteem.

Cord 2: Courage

In Joshua 1:9 God commands Joshua, 'Be strong and courageous! Do not be afraid or discouraged. For the LORD your God is with you wherever you go' (NLT). Joshua was having something of a perfectionistic crisis as he took over the leadership of the people of Israel from Moses. He felt unworthy, and thought it better to run away and hide in a shed than to take on the task and fail.

No doubt he was struggling with self-doubt as he tried to fill big shoes, and was desperate for the approval of the people who were now following him. What he needed was the courage to be himself, fully aware of his strengths and weaknesses, and fully trusting in God's promise.

Practising self-compassion (as opposed to perfectionism) is an act of *courage*. It is a decision to be authentically 'you' in the light of great pressure to perform or conform. As you courageously choose self-compassion, you defy

ecome more integrated into your normal life. Healthy habits
eap healthy benefits over the long haul.

Consider the first time you rode a bicycle. It was undoubt-
dly very wobbly and uncomfortable. You probably needed
o be very conscious of how to ride every time you attempted
. How about years later? Do you consciously think about
ow to ride your bike, or do you just do it automatically? (If
ou don't ride a bike, maybe consider swimming.) Compassion
perates in a very similar way, moving from being a deliberate
tivity to a very natural one, but you can greatly help this
rocess through practising every day.

Directly expressing compassion to ourselves and others is
ifficult task, but it can be hugely helped by becoming more
actised in engaging with compassion. The following three
ercises are created to help you to grow more comfortable
th compassion in your everyday life. You might find that
ere is one that particularly resonates with you. If so, we
ggest that you use that one regularly rather than worrying
out doing all three.

rcise: Compassion Home Base

ating a mental image that you can recall in times of
ss is a well-practised relaxation technique. Compassion
me Base is slightly different in that we are asking you to
ate a mental setting that represents compassion and
mth to you. Having established this image, you will then
ose to recall it at least once every day and in times where
feel provoked to use old perfectionistic coping
egies.

ou may find it helpful to write a description of your
ge first. Try to include as much sensory detail as possible.
(Will's) actual Compassion Home Base is described
w:

defensiveness. You take full responsibility for what is yours,
while encouraging (not discouraging) yourself to press on
towards your goals.

> Switch from berating yourself to encouraging yourself
> towards your goal.

Cord 3: Grace

In 2 Corinthians 12:9, Paul reports God saying to him, 'My
grace is sufficient for you, for my power is made perfect in
weakness.' While our perfectionism purports to be powerful,
true power comes through the interplay between our vulnerability and God's authority.

When we are loved, that's when we are dangerous. Grace
is the knowledge of the love of God for us despite our unworthiness, despite not matching up or deserving a reward.
This is why the Christian gospel is good news for perfectionists. The very economy of God's grace inverts the underpinning
principle of perfectionism: that you have to achieve to receive.
Grace says, 'While we were still sinners, Christ died for us'
(Romans 5:8).

Self-compassion could be described as agreeing with the
compassion of God for you, and what could be more life
changing than that? As my (Will's) favourite author Brennan
Manning puts it, 'Grace is sufficient even though we huff
and puff with all our might to try to find something or
someone it cannot cover. Grace is enough. He is enough. Jesus
is enough.'[9] Perfectionists will always need to remind themselves that God will never love you more because of your
achievements, but he will always love you because of
your very existence. There is nothing you can do to make
him love you more, and nothing you can do to make him love
you less.

defensiveness. You take full responsibility for what is yours, while encouraging (not discouraging) yourself to press on towards your goals.

> Switch from berating yourself to encouraging yourself towards your goal.

Cord 3: Grace

In 2 Corinthians 12:9, Paul reports God saying to him, 'My grace is sufficient for you, for my power is made perfect in weakness.' While our perfectionism purports to be powerful, true power comes through the interplay between our vulnerability and God's authority.

When we are loved, that's when we are dangerous. Grace is the knowledge of the love of God for us despite our unworthiness, despite not matching up or deserving a reward. This is why the Christian gospel is good news for perfectionists. The very economy of God's grace inverts the underpinning principle of perfectionism: that you have to achieve to receive. Grace says, 'While we were still sinners, Christ died for us' (Romans 5:8).

Self-compassion could be described as agreeing with the compassion of God for you, and what could be more life changing than that? As my (Will's) favourite author Brennan Manning puts it, 'Grace is sufficient even though we huff and puff with all our might to try to find something or someone it cannot cover. Grace is enough. He is enough. Jesus is enough.'[9] Perfectionists will always need to remind themselves that God will never love you more because of your achievements, but he will always love you because of your very existence. There is nothing you can do to make him love you more, and nothing you can do to make him love you less.

Exercise: Self-compassion

Find a comfortable and quiet place to sit for five minutes. Again, try to turn off any potential distractions.

Bring to mind a distant memory of a time when you tried but failed. It may be a time when you were running in a sports day race as a child, or sitting an exam or trying to achieve in an area in which you were not naturally gifted.

- Neutrally observe yourself at that time. What do you notice about your disposition?
- Using your new knowledge of perfectionism, what would you like to explain to your younger self?
- How do you imagine responding differently, had you known then what you know today?
- What would you say to your younger self about the courage to be who you are? How might that have changed your feelings at the time?
- Imagine you wrapped your younger self up in a big hug at this moment. What might that feel like?
- If you had the chance to whisper in your ear about grace, what would you tell your younger self?

Now take a moment to reflect upon the emotions that exercise has stirred up in you. You may like to take a walk outside or make yourself a hot drink. When you feel ready, return to pray the concluding prayer below:

Dear Lord God,
I give you thanks for me, with all my weaknesses and
*   vulnerabilities.*
I am mindful of your grace and love for me without condition.
I hand over my self-focused hostility to you.
I welcome your infinite compassion into my heart.

I pray that you might bless me with joy and peace at this
*   moment.*
In the name of your Son, Jesus Christ,
Amen

Following this exercise:

- Were you surprised by the strength of emotion you felt when engaging with your younger self? What did you notice about your tone when offering yourself advice and encouragement? Was it easy or difficult to act compassionately towards yourself? Did you feel undeserving?
- When you imagined hugging your younger self, what were your primary emotions? What did you feel in your own body?
- How did your interaction reflect Jesus' ministry of grace to you? How could you bring this compassionate practice into your day-to-day living?

Notes:

Compassion in your every day

You may have found the preceding activity very difficult or uncomfortable: if so, you did it right. Self-compassion is not the typical language of a person struggling with perfectionism, and just like any new skill, it takes time to master. The benefits of this sort of exercise build over time, and while the activities may initially feel contrived, they will gradually become more integrated into your normal life. Healthy habits reap healthy benefits over the long haul.

Consider the first time you rode a bicycle. It was undoubtedly very wobbly and uncomfortable. You probably needed to be very conscious of how to ride every time you attempted it. How about years later? Do you consciously think about how to ride your bike, or do you just do it automatically? (If you don't ride a bike, maybe consider swimming.) Compassion operates in a very similar way, moving from being a deliberate activity to a very natural one, but you can greatly help this process through practising every day.

Directly expressing compassion to ourselves and others is a difficult task, but it can be hugely helped by becoming more practised in engaging with compassion. The following three exercises are created to help you to grow more comfortable with compassion in your everyday life. You might find that there is one that particularly resonates with you. If so, we suggest that you use that one regularly rather than worrying about doing all three.

Exercise: Compassion Home Base

Creating a mental image that you can recall in times of stress is a well-practised relaxation technique. Compassion Home Base is slightly different in that we are asking you to create a mental setting that represents compassion and warmth to you. Having established this image, you will then choose to recall it at least once every day and in times where you feel provoked to use old perfectionistic coping strategies.

You may find it helpful to write a description of your image first. Try to include as much sensory detail as possible. My (Will's) actual Compassion Home Base is described below:

'Standing behind the warm grill of a beach-side café, I slowly cook eggs and bacon. I can see the breaking waves of the sea in front of me, plastic inflatables flapping in the wind on either side of the hatch, and bright buckets and spades filling the counter top. I can smell the breakfast mixed with the fresh salty sea air. I feel safe. I am precious to God just as I am. I am valuable. I do not need to strive. God is with me.'

My Compassion Home Base:

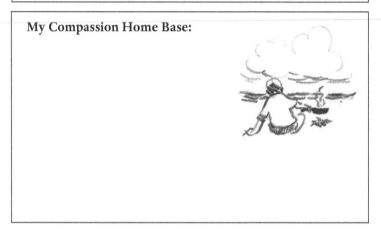

Exercise: Compassion postcard

Writing in a compassionate and connected way is an excellent way of practising compassion. It also gives you the added benefit of concretely reviewing your compassionate feelings and thoughts.

Try to write a compassionate postcard to yourself, using the three compassion attributes we discussed earlier: knowledge, courage and grace. Regard your current circumstances, and offer yourself non-judgmental and supportive encouragement. Remember that the tone of your writing is as important as the message. You may try extending this exercise to people other than yourself, despite not actually sending the card.

Exercise: Compassion prayer

You can pray anywhere and at any time. Not only does God respond to your prayers, but praying will also transform you. Compassionate prayer is a foundation stone to overcoming perfectionism, and one of the most dynamic tools for building compassion for yourself and others.

Perfectionism can also influence our prayer lives, making us more conscious of getting through a list than resting in the presence of God. One way in which the early monastic tradition overcame this issue was to pray simply, repetitively, and to incorporate breathing as a part of their prayer.

Probably the most famous early form of such prayers is the Jesus Prayer, which we wrote about in chapter 7. Remember that this prayer helps us engage with the compassionate heart of God; it is a prayer that changes us, one that makes God's salvation real to our hearts rather than just our heads. It is a space where we can pray without overthinking (or even being perfectionistic), and instead rest in God's presence and in the confidence of a salvation we have already received through Jesus' death and resurrection. 'The power of the Jesus Prayer is rooted in a conviction that God's presence is trans-formative. When people are around God, they are changed.'[10] We suggest that you use our compassion-focused version of this prayer as a daily practice for compassion:

'Lord Jesus Christ, Son of God,
Have compassion on me, a sinner.'

Pray the first line of the prayer while drawing in a breath and pray the second line through your out-breath. We suggest that you might pray this prayer repetitively in blocks of as many as twenty-five recitations (please remain flexible and encouraging here). This practice can take place anywhere during your day: walking to work, sitting in a park or in any quiet space.

The central purpose of repeating the prayer in this way is to lead you through the three stages of prayer, from oral repetition, to content focus, to heart transformation.[11] The use of this style of prayer is particularly powerful in bypassing the rational, task-orientated mind and speaking really directly to the heart. Ultimately, experiencing the compassion of God through Christ to your heart will transform your relationship with God, yourself and others.

Summary

Compassion sounds like something that should flow from the heart – and so it does – but it is also something that can be learned and practised and embedded. Please don't fall into the trap of just waiting for this to 'happen', but put in the hard graft of the things suggested in this chapter and the exercises that follow. Practising compassion may feel contrived, but it will become natural over time. Not only will your relationships with others benefit, but your emotional health and your ability to engage in God's grace for you will also increase.

More exercises

1. What was your first reaction to the idea of practising compassion to yourself?
2. How strongly did you equate compassion to reward? How easy was it to be compassionate to someone who you felt was undeserving?
3. What did you learn about yourself through practising self-compassion? What did you learn about how God feels about you?

4. Which of the everyday compassion exercises did you find most helpful? How will you incorporate it into your daily life?

AFTERWORD: JOURNEYING FORWARD

We must be willing to fail and to appreciate the truth that often 'Life is not a problem to be solved, but a mystery to be lived'.

(M. Scott Peck)

Maintaining the gains you have made over perfectionism takes commitment. Remember that the problem of perfection is multifaceted and includes a 'dispositional' element. This means that should your circumstances become particularly pressured in the future, you may find yourself falling back into these negative and self-defeating behaviours. However, the work we have done means that you now have the ability to choose more supportive, thankful and compassionate approaches to living. The more you make decisions to challenge your old perfectionistic beliefs, the more natural and automatic your new supportive behaviours and outlooks will be. At the very root of this ongoing journey is an active decision towards a greater level of vulnerability in which we commit to being more honest about our weaknesses, both with others and with ourselves.

Kintsukuroi is a historical Japanese craft in which broken ceramics are repaired with powdered silver or gold resin.

Tradition has it that in the fifteenth century, a cracked Chinese tea bowl was uniquely repaired by a Japanese craftsman. His gold repair, which followed the contours of the fracture, was so beautiful that it gave birth to a form of art in which the flaws in broken pottery were celebrated rather than disguised.

In 2 Corinthians 4:7 Paul writes, 'We have this treasure in jars of clay, to show that the surpassing power belongs to God and not to us.' Just like in the *Kintsukuroi* bowl, God's power is revealed in the brokenness of our lives, our struggles and our weaknesses.

Perfectionism attempts to hide our vulnerabilities, offering others the illusion that we are in complete control. It leaves us believing that life is a problem we can solve. It leaves us living a life of anxiety, always worried about our performance or approval. As David says in Psalm 31:12, 'I have become like a broken vessel', and despite our best perfectionistic efforts, we cannot fix ourselves.

God, however, can mend our hearts and minds if we decide to trust and rest in his 'surpassing power'. His compassion in our brokenness becomes the mark of real beauty and a living sign that we have been made truly acceptable despite (and not because of) all of our human effort.

Grace journey

The exercises and insights that we have shared with you over the last eight chapters will provide you with many of the tools and insights that you need to live more freely. However, Rob and I want to leave you with an awareness that the 'surpassing power' that Paul is referencing is not limited to our earthly lives.

At the heart of the Bible is the message of grace, a sweet medicine for all people, not least for perfectionists. It is beautifully encapsulated in Romans 5:8: 'But God shows his love for us in that while we were still sinners, Christ died for us.'

We talked about the reward principle in chapter 8, an underpinning feature in the lives of many perfectionists. Yet the message of the Bible is that 'while we were *still* sinners, Christ died for us'. God's love for us was unmerited, and that continues to be the case. There is nothing we can do, no way we can perform, that can increase the depths of his love.

The two archers

As hard as we try, and as close to perfect as we can make it, our lives are still marked by sin. Think about two archers: one is a perfectionist and one is just a bad archer, and they have come to hit a target before the king. The perfectionist arrives early, does lots of stretches, measures wind speed and the distance to the target. The bad archer arrives late and looks like he has just rolled out of bed.

The perfectionist goes through a great routine, stretching and aiming before letting his arrow fly. It lands just a millimetre from the target. The bad archer lets his arrow fly without even looking at the target. It lands in the adjacent field, narrowly missing a sheep.

However you look at it, both archers missed the target.

The message of the Bible is that all of us have missed the target, some by an inch and some by a mile. The truth is we all need a saviour to rescue us and make us acceptable to a holy God. Rob and I both believe that Jesus Christ is the Saviour that we need. John 3:16 says, 'For God so loved the world, that he gave his only Son, that whoever believes in him should not perish but have eternal life.'

This is the message of grace. It is the undeserved sacrifice of God for our own sakes, simply because he loves us. This grace offers us a life with God now, but it also offers us an eternal life with him when we die. All we need to do to receive this grace is to accept that God did this saving work for us and welcome Jesus into our hearts. If you would like to take this step, you might like to pray the prayer below.

Accepting Jesus prayer

Dear Lord Jesus Christ,

I give you thanks and praise, that because of your great sacrifice for me, I have been made acceptable to God. I recognize that this is not a product of my efforts or achievements, but a pure gift of your grace and compassion. As a broken vessel, I resign to you my desire to repair myself. I lay down the rod of perfectionism and instead invite your compassion to overwhelm me.

I welcome your healing power to come into the wounds of my past and the habits of my present. May the scars radiate your beauty and be a sign of your grace to those around me. Give me the strength in the months ahead to continue to practise gratitude and compassion so that my life would become rich in worship. I thank you again for unmerited grace. May it become the beat that I walk to.

Amen

The grace list

It is not too difficult to see what an impact living life in the light of God's grace will have on a perfectionist. Also, please tell someone about this life-changing event. Living your life in the light of a God who loves you unconditionally undermines so many of the assumptions that keep perfectionism alive. Equally, we believe that there is no fuller nor more wonderful way to live than in relationship with our Creator and Redeemer.

If you would like to explore faith for the first time, or would like to refresh your faith, we would really recommend that you consider attending an Alpha course or Christianity Explored course through your local church. See www.alpha.org and www.christianityexplored.org.

You may find this helpful to read every day for a month after completing this book:

I didn't earn God's grace; it was God's unmerited gift to me because he loves me.

I am not in control of my life or my future; God is.

When I make mistakes, Jesus' sacrifice on the cross covers them all.

Nothing can separate me for the love of God in Christ Jesus.

I am not ruled by the opinions of others. I am here to serve God.

Jesus' compassion to me is boundless. I will direct his compassion to myself and others.

My life is an act of worship to God; I will live a life marked by gratitude.

My identity is secure as a child of God; nothing can take that away from me.

I am forgiven for all my sins through Jesus Christ. I am free.

God is in my character, not my performance.

APPENDIX 1: PRAYERS AND MEDITATIONS

The Perfectionist's Prayer, once more (when you need to be reminded of grace)

Dear Lord Jesus Christ,

I give you thanks and praise, that because of your great sacrifice for me I have been made acceptable to God. I recognize that this is not a product of my efforts or achievements, but a pure gift of your grace and compassion. As a broken vessel, I resign to you my desire to repair myself. I lay down the rod of perfectionism and instead invite your compassion to overwhelm me. I welcome your healing power to come into the wounds of my past and the habits of my present. May the scars radiate your beauty and be a sign of your grace to those around me. Give me the strength in the months ahead to continue to practise gratitude and compassion so that my life would become rich in worship. I thank you again for unmerited grace. May it become the beat that I walk to.

Amen

The compassion prayer (for times of self-criticism and self-attack)

Lord God,

You created me and you know me.

You have made me in your image and have loved me with an
everlasting love.

When I have turned my back on you, you have turned your
face towards me.

When I have stumbled to the floor, you have restored my
dignity.

When I have been full of criticism, you have been full of
compassion for me.

As I am tempted to agree with the enemies' accusations
against me,

let me hear your voice of love.

I put the weapon words I would use against myself down
before you.

I pick up your words of acceptance, comfort, love and
patience.

I choose to treat myself as you treat me and as my neighbour
would wish to be treated.

In Jesus' name,

Amen

Prayer for when stress is taking over

Lord Jesus Christ,
I have need of you and you alone.
I will not fear man, nor reputation, nor standard. I will fear
the Lord.
I am at your disposal; you are not at mine.
I am who I am because you are who you are.
Nothing can make me more of the creation that you spoke
into being.
I will never be more acceptable than Christ's blood can
make me.
I choose the priority of God over the priority of the world.
If the world sees me to fail, I care not.
I will give only my best and nothing more.
My satisfaction is in Christ and Christ alone.
Amen

APPENDIX 2: MORE PRACTICAL HELP

This section contains some extra material that will help you go deeper. It is not essential, but it may help answer some questions you have along the way, and will direct those of you who need it to more resources and help.

What is the cognitive behavioural approach?

Cognitive behavioural therapy, or CBT, was first clearly outlined by an American psychiatrist and psychoanalyst called Aaron T. Beck. As a psychoanalyst, he spent a lot of his time trying to interpret and discover his patients' unconscious defence mechanisms and anxieties. However, it occurred to him one day that it might be easier actually to ask the person what thoughts were in their head. This is not to say that psychoanalysis is no good (it is very good for some types of problems), but for many common mental health problems, CBT has been found to be the most effective form of therapy, and is the one most often recommended by the NHS. At its core is asking about thoughts: what went through your mind, what did you think next, how does this thought relate to this other different thought, and so on. CBT never asks the *why* question, although you often end up realizing why yourself.

As well as thoughts, it looks at behaviours, especially avoidant behaviours and those times when you have escaped from a situation. CBT therapists are also interested in the more subtle 'safety' behaviours that allow you to keep on going in an anxious situation while never fully helping, and actually making the problem worse in the long term.

The idea is that by changing unhelpful thoughts and modifying unhelpful and cyclical behaviours, then you will be able to help the person's mood. This typically takes around twelve sessions: two or three for helping the person understand their problem, two or three to get more evidence about how to change, three to six for changing, and two or three for making sure things are really fixed and that you know what you need to keep on doing in the future. Some simple phobias will be quicker; some more complex anxieties and ruminations (including severe perfectionism) can take up to thirty sessions. The sessions are typically weekly or fortnightly and an hour long.

Find out more about CBT and find a local accredited therapist at www.babcp.com.

What to do when perfectionism really takes hold

Self-help books like this one are really helpful, especially if you read them alongside a friend or relative who can help you think through what they are asking and enable you to stay on track. However, they are the *most simple* level of intervention. There will be some people who need more help with their perfectionism, and this might include seeing your GP, seeing a therapist (preferably a CBT therapist), and even seeing a psychiatrist and taking medication if you are clinically depressed.

All this sounds a bit scary, which is why this section contains resources to help you find the right person to talk to. Remember, all of these people do these jobs because they want to help people who struggle with their mental health, and they may even have had such problems themselves. However, if you are cautious, it is absolutely fine for you to take someone along for the consultation and explain that you would like them to sit in, at least for the beginning. As a psychiatrist, I (Rob) know how grateful I am when people bring someone along to the consultation, as it lets me know the person has support, and also that they are more likely to remember what I say.

Seeing a therapist

If this book really resonates with you, and you think you need more help, we would recommend that you see your GP and ask them to refer you on. We would also say that you are better off seeing a secular therapist who is good rather than a Christian therapist who is not so good. Maybe you can find a good Christian one, although sometimes it is helpful to see someone who does not share your faith, as you really have to examine many of your assumptions that may have been unwittingly keeping the problems going.

We would recommend seeing a cognitive behavioural therapist if you have ongoing and chronic perfectionism. A number of other types of therapy can help in this area, and these include person-centred therapy or psychodynamic therapy. However, it is CBT which has the most research evidence for effectively treating depression and which is the basis for this book. The national association of accredited CBT therapists, all of whom have trained to post-graduate diploma level, is the British Association of Behavioural and Cognitive

Psychotherapists. You can find out more at www.babcp.com and follow the links to www.cbtregisteruk.com or by calling BABCP on 0161 705 4304.

Getting urgent help

There are times when you need to talk to someone *now*, and the list below gives you the relevant telephone numbers.

NHS Choices (England and Wales)	Twenty-four-hour advice for people in England and Wales Call the new non-emergency number of 111 www.nhs.uk
NHS 24 (for Scotland)	Twenty-four-hour advice for people in Scotland Call the new non-emergency number of 111 www.nhs24.com
Lifeline (for Northern Ireland)	If you are feeling suicidal – 0808 808 8000
Your local A&E/ Casualty/ER	These are open twenty-four hours a day, and you can just walk in if it is a genuine emergency. Remember, not all hospitals have an A&E department. Look for the red sign.
Call 999	In a real emergency, when you cannot get to the hospital, you can call 999 from any phone and ask for an ambulance.

What to do if you start slipping backwards

Over the next few months, we hope that you will continue to grow more and more in how you manage perfectionism and how you enjoy life. However, this journey is unlikely to be totally smooth. There are going to be some bumps and wiggles along the way.

How we react when a setback comes along can make all the difference. If we are able to roll with the punches a bit, this can mean that we can ride over these setbacks. If, however, we panic and overreact, and predict that this will result in a disaster, this can turn the setback into a genuine disaster, and we can be back at square one.

This list is something you should read if you are having a bit of a bumpy ride. We hope it will keep your thinking on track and mean that the bump will only be a bump and not a disaster. Take the time to make some notes about what you feel about each tip.

	Practical tips	Your notes
1	You know that setbacks are likely to occur. This was likely to happen at some point.	
2	Setbacks are temporary and short-term hiccups, and will usually settle after a few days.	
3	Setbacks do not mean disasters or that you are back to square one.	
4	A setback can be a positive experience, allowing you to build on the skills you have learned.	
5	Setbacks can be predicted. Identify some situations where they might occur.	
6	Do not avoid whatever caused the setback. This needs to be dealt with.	

	Practical tips	Your notes
7	Do not escape from the situation by leaving or drinking alcohol. It *will* settle with time.	
8	You have learned a range of skills during your reading of this book. Use them now, or read through your notes.	
9	Set yourself targets to get back on track. Start off with some short-term ones to get you to tomorrow.	
10	If you have tried all of these, talk to someone who will be able to give you good advice. Whom will you talk to?	

Keep a note here of situations where you might be likely to have a setback:

Keep a note here of what you did when you met with a setback and what happened:

APPENDIX 3: OTHER BOOKS ABOUT PERFECTIONISM

Christian books
Perfecting Ourselves To Death, Richard Winter, ISBN 9780830832590
Dr Winter shares some ground with our book, but with less structure and fewer exercises. There is more discussion about perfectionism in modern society and history (both church and general). The strong emphasis on grace gives a clear goal for the Christian mind.

Freedom To Be Your Best, Ashley Null, ISBN 9783775139663
Sports Chaplain Ashley Null shares stories of his work with many Olympic-level athletes as they have to deal with both losing (what went wrong?) and winning (what next?). A relationship with Jesus is the answer to many of the struggles, and this is clearly unpacked.

Insight into Perfectionism (Waverley Guides), Chris Ledger and Wendy Bray, ISBN 9781853455063
This short guide is part of the Waverley Abbey series for counsellors. The material is good, but necessarily brief. The book is full of helpful practical pointers and biblical reflections.

Secular books

Overcoming Perfectionism, Roz Shafran, Sarah Egan and Tracey Wade, ISBN 9781845197428
This is the best secular book on the subject, heavily based on CBT principles and with many exercises to help you change. It is the next-best thing to seeing a CBT therapist and covers the how-to-change angle in more detail than we could.

When Perfect Isn't Good Enough, Martin Anthony and Richard Swainson, ISBN 9781572245594
One of the classics and now in its second edition, this American text is also CBT-based, but with more descriptions and a wider range of examples. This is less about clinical perfectionism (those who are struggling), but also for those who still seem to be succeeding.

The Gift of Imperfection, Brené Brown, ISBN 9781592858491
American writer and TED speaker Brené Brown shares many stories and tips for dealing with perfectionism. It is the easiest to read of all the books we have recommended, but it is still a tough journey. She writes as a Christian, but for a mainstream/secular audience.

NOTES

Introduction

1. Samuel Johnson, *Lives of the English Poets* (1781).
2. Vanuatu, Solomon Islands, Fiji and Papua New Guinea.
3. www.scientificamerican.com/article/1959-cargo-cults-melanesia/?page=1.
4. http://rationalwiki.org/wiki/Cargo_cult.
5. This definition is based on a number of books on perfectionism, which are listed in Appendix 3.
6. Corin Pilling, Assistant Director, Livability UK.
7. A number of researchers are working in this area, including Roz Shafran, Sarah Egan and Tracey Wade, whose book *Overcoming Perfectionism* is referenced in Appendix 3.
8. Joshua 3.
9. Exodus 33:3.

1. Perfectionism – good or bad?

1. Anne Wilson Schaef (1990), *Meditations for Women Who Do Too Much* (republished by HarperOne, 2006).

2. Brené Brown, *The Gift of Imperfections: Let Go of Who You Think You're Supposed to Be and Embrace Who You Are* (Hazelden Information & Educational Services, 2010).

3. P. L. Hewitt and G. L. Flett (1990), 'Perfectionism and depression: a multidimensional analysis', *Journal of Social Behaviour and Personality*, 5: 423–438.

4. M. W. Enns and B. J. Cox (2002), 'The nature and assessment of perfectionism: a critical analysis', in G. L. Flett and P. L. Hewitt (eds), *Perfectionism* (pp. 33–62). Washington, DC: American Psychological Association.

5. Anne Lamott, *Some Instructions on Writing and Life* (Random House, 1994).

6. www.asa.org.uk/Rulings/Adjudications/2015/7/Protein-World-Ltd/SHP_ADJ_300099.aspx.

7. Attributed: www.new-wine.org/sites/default/files/resources/download//2015//01/rta15-gratitude-bundle4.pdf.

8. www.nhs.uk/Conditions/body-dysmorphia/Pages/Introduction.aspx.

9. www.psychcentral.com.

2. Perfectionism and faith

1. Charles Stanley, *The Spirit-filled Life: Discover the Joy of Surrendering to the Holy Spirit* (Thomas Nelson, New York, 2014), p. 6.

2. Brené Brown, *The Gifts of Imperfection*.

3. Readers may wish to look at the use of *telios* in Colossians 1:28, Colossians 4:12, Ephesians 4:13–14 and James 1:8. See also the Hebrew word *tamin* in Job 1:1 and Psalm 101:2.

4. There have been many times throughout church history when the pursuit of holiness has come unhealthily to the fore. Perhaps the best example is some of the teachings of John Wesley, exemplified in his book *Plain Account of Christian Perfection* and a hymn line: 'he walks in glorious liberty, to sin entirely dead'. These teachings, and others from around that time, go under

the general name of the Holiness Movement, which triggered Bishop J. C. Ryle's classic book *Holiness* as a corrective. They can be traced back to gnostic errors in theology, which are dealt with in the New Testament. For a good overview of incorrect teaching about holiness, see the Appendix in Richard Winter's book, *Perfecting Ourselves to Death* (IVP USA, 2005).

5. C. S. Lewis, *Mere Christianity* (William Collins, 2012).
6. B. Brown, *Daring Greatly: How the Courage To Be Vulnerable Transforms the Way We Live, Love, Parent and Lead* (Penguin, New York, 2014).

3. Perfectionism and personality

1. Alister McGrath's book on C. S. Lewis (*C. S. Lewis – A Life: Eccentric Genius, Reluctant Prophet*) contains a section on Tolkien (p. 199): 'Although Tolkien was a storyteller, he took his role as a "subcreator" with great seriousness, devising complex histories and languages, and populating his novels with characters whose roots went deep into the stories of Middle Earth. Inevitably, Tolkien found himself overwhelmed with the need to maintain consistency, ensuring the proper correlation of his complicated and detailed backstory and the written narrative. Each leaf on the "tree of stories" had to be just right – a process which inevitably made the achievement of consistency triumph over imaginative subcreation. Tolkien became trapped in his own complex world, unable to complete it because of his anxieties about the coherence and consistency of what he had already written. His fussiness threatened to overwhelm his creativity.'
2. You can read more about the 'Big Five' at http://en.wikipedia.org/wiki/Big_Five_personality_traits, and you can take an online test at www.personalitytest.org.uk.
3. D. J. Ozer and V. Benet-Martínez (2006), 'Personality and the prediction of consequential outcomes', *Annual Review of Psychology*, 57: 401–421.

4. J. Moser, J. D. Slane, B. S. Alexandra and K. L. Klump (2012), 'Etiologic relationships between anxiety and dimensions of maladaptive perfectionism in young adult female twins', *Depression and Anxiety*, Jan; 29(1): 47–53.

5. André Agassi, *Open* (HarperCollins, New York, 2011).

6. Reproduced from http://genius.com/Andre-agassi-open-annotated.

7. The psychoanalysists often came up with rather sexual-sounding metaphors for human development. This is not because they are being rude, but because these visceral feelings are the way a small child develops. In adults, especially if there has been a trauma at the relevant stage in development, the stages are repeated or you can become 'fixed' (hence the phrase 'anal fixation') in a particular pattern of behaviour. The good news is that this is not a permanent state; development and growth to a mature way of being is always possible.

8. See Appendix 3 for full information about this book. The table is on p. 18. Used with permission.

9. A simple scale for self-esteem can be found at http://personality-testing.info/tests/RSE.php. This is based on the Rosenberg Self-esteem Scale and allows you to see how your score compares with those of the general population.

10. See http://en.wikipedia.org/wiki/Narcissus_(mythology) for the full story.

11. If you think you might be suffering from OCD, it is essential to get professional help as your condition will not go away on its own. Three of the best places to start are www.ocdaction.org.uk, www.ocduk.org and www.ocdonline.com.

12. Details on how to get help in an emergency are given in Appendix 2.

13. R. Winter, *Perfecting Ourselves to Death* (IVP Books, Illinois, 2005), p. 13.

4. Changing your mind

1. V. Frankl, *Man's Search for Meaning* (Rider and Co., 1946).

2. www.entepreneur.com/article/224509.

3. With thanks to Reverend Ashley Null for this study. Read his book on working with Olympic-level athletes and perfectionism called *Real Joy: Freedom To Be Your Best* (Hanssler, Germany, 2004).

4. See more at www.imdb.com/title/tt0314331.

5. R. Shafran, Z. Cooper and C. G. Fairburn (2002), 'Clinical perfectionism: a cognitive-behavioural analysis', *Behaviour Research and Therapy*, 40: 773–791, and C. Riley and R. Shafran (2005), 'Clinical perfectionism: a preliminary qualitative analysis', *Behavioural and Cognitive Psychotherapy*, 33(3): 369–374.

6. Quoted by Lorne A. Adrian in *The Most Important Thing I Know* (Andrews McMeel, 2001).

7. See http://en.wikipedia.org/wiki/First_impression_(psychology) for a summary of this.

8. See Daniel J. Simons' research from the University of Illinois at www.psychology.illinois.edu/people/dsimons. You can learn more about his best-selling book at www.theinvisiblegorilla.com.

9. D. C. Steinmetz, *Luther in Context* (Baker Books, Grand Rapids, 1995), p. 2.

10. J. Kittleson, *Luther the Reformer* (Augsburg, Minneapolis, 1986), p. 287.

5. Changing your reality

1. M. Jackson, *Moonwalk* (Doubleday, 1988).

2. The website www.accesscreditcard.info charts the history of the card. The advertising was not that successful, with Access ultimately being bought out by MasterCard™.

3. R. Nozick, *Anarchy, State and Utopia* (Basic Books, 1977).

4. www.michaelhyatt.com.

5. In interview with WVDH, October 2015.

6. K. L. Ladd and B. Spika (2002), 'Inward, outward, upward: cognitive aspects of prayer', *Journal for the Scientific Study of Religion*, 41(3): 475–484.

7. D. Gibson (1983), 'The obsessive personality and the evangelical', *Journal of Psychology and Christianity*, 2(3): 32–33.

8. G. K. Chesterton, *What's Wrong With the World?* (Forgotten Books, 1910), pt 4, ch. 14.

6. Achieving excellence

1. J. Piper, *Desiring God: Meditations of a Christian Hedonist* (IVP, Leicester, 1986).

2. A. Null (2008), 'Finding the right place: professional sport as a Christian vocation'. Published in Donald Deardorff and John White (eds), *The Image of God in the Human Body: Essays on Christianity and Sports* (Edwin Mellon Press, Lewiston, 2008). Used with permission of the author.

3. We are indebted to the Reverend Dr Ashley Null for many of the ideas and illustrations in this chapter, for both their use in this book and their ministry in our own lives.

4. Null, ibid.

5. Tony Ladd and James A. Mathisen, *Muscular Christianity: Evangelical Protestants and the Development of American Sport* (Baker, Grand Rapids, 1999), p. 80.

6. H. Richard Niebuhr, *Christ and Culture* (Harper & Brothers, New York, 1951) pp. 45–82.

7. Niebuhr, *Christ and Culture*, pp. 149–189, especially pp. 170–179; Gustaf Wingren, *Luther on Vocation*, trans. Carl C. Rasmussen (Muhlenberg Press, Philadelphia, 1957), pp. 27–29.

8. Gustaf Wingren, *Luther on Vocation*, pp. 27–29.

9. See www.channel4.com/programmes/the-secret-millionaire.

10. Null, ibid.

11. Nick Land has written about this approach to medical leadership here: www.cmf.org.uk/publications/content.asp?context=article&id=26316.

12. Ashley Null has written a book on this topic called *Real Joy: Freedom To Be Your Best* (Hanssler, Germany, 1996).

13. Null, ibid.

14. Neilson Holidays: www.neilson.co.uk.

15. My limited bookshelf of systematic theology is: W. Gruden, *Bible Doctrine* (IVP, Leicester, 1999); T. C. Hammond, *In Understanding Be Men* (IVP, Leicester, 1968); B. Milne, *Know the Truth* (IVP, Leicester, 1998).

16. Shelly Millar, 'Reclaiming Sabbath', *Premier Youthwork Magazine*, October 2015, pp. 31–33.

17. http://billygraham.org/story/bubba-watson-showing-the-light.

7. Practising gratitude

1. Attributed to Meister Eckhart, a thirteenth-century mystic.

2. Cited in Robert Burton's 1621 *Anatomy of Melancholy*.

3. See the description and references at https://en.wikipedia.org/wiki/Hedonic_treadmill.

4. P. Brickman, D. Coates and R. Janoff-Bulman (1978), 'Lottery winners and accident victims: is happiness relative?', *Journal of Personality and Social Psychology*, 36(8): 917–927.

5. In interview with WVDH, October 2015; see www.rowforfreedom.com.

6. For an introduction to 'Positive Psychology – the Science of Happiness', see T. Ben-Shahar, *Happier* (McGraw Hill, 2008). For the specific references for hedonic adaptation, see S. Frederick, G. Loewenstein, D. Kahneman, E. Deiner and N. Schwarz (1999), *Well-being: The Foundations of Hedonic Psychology* (Russell Sage Foundation, New York, 1999), pp. 302–329.

7. R. A. Emmons, *Thanks!: How the New Science of Gratitude Can Make You Happier* (Houghton Mifflin Company, 2007), p. 2.

8. Augustine of Hippo (AD 354–430), *Confessions*. Book 1, Part 1.

9. See http://qbible.com/hebrew-old-testament/psalms/91.html.

10. Sat-nav perfectionism occurs irrespective of the gender you set it to!

8. Practising compassion

1. From an essay on peace: www.beliefnet.com/Inspiration/2004/04/Desmond-Tutus-Recipe-For-Peace.aspx.

2. www.psychologicalscience.org/index.php/news/releases/compassion-training.html.

3. D. Kelntner and J. L. Goetz (2007), 'Compassion', in R. F. Baumeister and K. D. Vols (eds), *Encyclopaedia of Social Psychology* (Sage), pp. 159–161.

4. H. Y. Weng, A. S. Fox *et al.* (2013), 'Compassion training alters altruism and neural responses to suffering', *Psychological Science*, May.

5. O. M. Klimecki, S. Leiberg, C. Lamm and T. Singer (2013), 'Functional neural plasticity and associated changes in positive affect after compassion training', *Cerebral Cortex*, 23(7): 1552–1561.

6. P. Gilbert, *Training Our Minds In, With and For Compassion* (Compassionate Mind Foundation, 2010).

7. We have written about Guilt Induction Parenting in one of our other books: *The Guilt Book* (IVP, 2014).

8. C. Germer, *The Mindful Path to Self Compassion: Freeing Yourself from Destructive Thoughts and Emotions* (Guilford Press, 2009).

9. B. Manning, *All is Grace: A Ragamuffin Memoir* (David C. Cook reprint, 2015).

10. www.patheos.com/blogs/billykangas/2011/10/praying-the-jesus-prayer.html.

11. These stages of prayer were first written down by Theophan the Recluse, a Russian Orthodox priest from the nineteenth century. See www.theophan.net for more information.

ABOUT THE MIND AND SOUL FOUNDATION

The Mind and Soul Foundation is a national networking, equipping and encouraging organization for people who are interested in how Christianity and mental health problems relate.

We have three main aims:

1. to network people across the UK who are interested in Christianity and mental health
2. to create high-quality resources for the church on this topic
3. to share information about what is already going on near you.

Some of our resources are:

- major annual conferences with high-quality speakers and seminars
- databases of Christian counsellors, mental health projects and mental-health-friendly churches across the UK

- over 400 articles on a wide range of topics
- regular emails highlighting new resources
- audio and video archive of over 150 talks.

www.mindandsoulfoundation.org

Real, inspiring and practical help from guys who really walk the talk.
Bear Grylls, Survivalist and Adventurer

This is more than a book about perfectionism; it is a guide to living a life full of thankfulness and kindness. Insightful and filled with practical wisdom, *The Perfectionism Book* is bound to change your life for the better.
Miranda Hart, Actress and Comedienne

Running a successful business is hindered not helped by perfectionism. Will and Rob give you the tools to achieve your dreams without the self-punishment.
Mark and Liz Warom, Founders and Directors, Temple Spa

Perfectionism is a disease that robs us of the fullness of life we were made for. This brilliant book explains the disease clearly, describes the symptoms, and points to the practices and patterns in which a remedy can be found. For those like me who are tired of living with this disease and are hungry for healing, there is no other book I'd want to place in your hand.
Pete Hughes, Vicar of KXC, London

In this latest book, Will and Rob passionately yet compassionately tackle the stealthy issue of perfectionism (a seemingly innocuous trait), and expose the price that our souls, our health and our relationships pay when in its grip. But they don't stop there. Rob and Will are unwilling to leave us with simply an awareness of our perfectionism. They share practical tools, strategies and prayers that break old patterns, speak life and truth to weary hearts, and lead us forward and guide us to a different kind of life. Take the time to read this book, because it has the potential to transform your quest for 'the perfect life' into a more whole, healthy, and altogether more fulfilling one.
Jo Saxton, Pastor, Mission Point Church and Chair of the Board, 3D Movements

The
Perfectionism
Book

The Perfectionism Book

Walking the path to freedom

Will van der Hart & Rob Waller

INTER-VARSITY PRESS
36 Causton Street, London SW1P 4ST, England
Email: ivp@ivpbooks.com
Website: www.ivpbooks.com

First published 2016
Reprinted 2017

British Library Cataloguing in Publication Data
A catalogue record for this book is available from the British Library.

ISBN: 978–1–78359–401–6
eBook ISBN: 978–1–78359–402–3

Set in Dante 12/15pt
Illustrated by Charlie Mackesy
Typeset in Great Britain by CRB Associates, Potterhanworth, Lincolnshire
Printed and bound in Great Britain by Ashford Colour Press Ltd, Gosport,
Hampshire

To those who excel.

CONTENTS

Acknowledgments   11
Foreword   13
Introduction   17

1. Perfectionism – good or bad?   25
2. Perfectionism and faith   41
3. Perfectionism and personality   57
4. Changing your mind   69
5. Changing your reality   87
6. Achieving excellence   103
7. Practising gratitude   117
8. Practising compassion   135

Afterword: Journeying forward   155

Appendix 1: Prayers and meditations   161
Appendix 2: More practical help   165
Appendix 3: Other books about perfectionism   171

Notes   173

ACKNOWLEDGMENTS

Rob would like to thank NHS Lothian for their continued support throughout his employment and training. Will would like to thank Patrick Regan and Charlie Mackesy for the insightful conversations that informed so much of this text. Thanks too to Shaun Lambert, Ashley Null and Roger Bretherton for their guidance, and to Charlotte Mulford and Lynn Mooreland for their guest editorial work. Special thanks to the editorial and marketing team at IVP (particularly Eleanor Trotter) for their skill and patience in working with our many drafts, and also for sharing our vision for this book. We would also like to thank those who have written commendations, Jo Rice for her foreword and Ben Dewhirst for his perspective as a teacher.

We are both indebted to our wives, Susanna and Lucinda, and to our families far more than we can say, and of course to our God who has taught us much about achievement and how to excel in his grace.